KU-716-380

CRUISE BOOK

Expert Advice for
Planning and Enjoying
a Perfect Vacation at Sea

Fourth Edition

~~~ JIM WEST ~~~

gpp

travel

Guilford, Connecticut

Copyright © 1998, 1999, 2003, 2008 by Jim West

ALL RIGHTS RESERVED. No part of this book may be reproduced or
transmitted in any form by any means, electronic or mechanical,
including photocopying and recording, or by any information
storage and retrieval system, except as may be expressly permitted
in writing from the publisher. Requests for permission should be
addressed to The Globe Pequot Press, Attn: Rights and Permissions
Department, P.O. Box 480, Guilford CT 06437.

Revised and updated by Ann Carroll Burgess
Text design by Georgiana Goodwin

ISBN 978-0-7627-4886-0

Printed in China
10 9 8 7 6 5 4 3 2 1

Contents

Introduction

How many times have you asked yourself "How do we …?" on a vacation or "if only we had known this before we left home!"

How do you discover the answers to those questions before you set sail? Ask questions, and more questions, and even more questions. Ask your travel agent. Ask friends who have cruised. You can even ask a cruise line questions. That's the secret to a perfect cruise: Ask the questions that matter to you. That's what this book is about, providing answers to frequently asked questions and concerns.

Choosing the perfect cruise for you depends highly on your knowing what is important to you in a vacation. Your friends may rave about the champagne cocktails at the captain's formal reception, but if you like to drink beer from the comfort of a deck chair, their recommendations will not be right for you. Do you want the adventure of new ports and places? Don't choose an itinerary with too many days at sea. Are you planning on taking your children? Make sure there is an established children's program with the ship's equivalent of "camp counselors." Are you wary of becoming seasick? Ask your travel agent to book you a cabin on a lower deck in the center of the ship. Are some of these questions that you didn't think to ask? Then please keep reading, as there are lots of secrets to finding the perfect cruise just for you.

Cruise lines vary greatly in style and personality. Each and every voyage is different: The officers, staff, and crew onboard the ship; the passenger mix sailing on that specific voyage; weather conditions; and even the ship itself all combine to make each sailing a unique experience.

First Things First: Choosing a Cruise

MILLIONS OF PEOPLE have already experienced the joy of going on a cruise. Cruise lines offer a dizzying array of cruise "products" today, and it takes only the skilled juggling of a travel planner to match your personality and budget with the cruise line, cruise ship, and itinerary that suit your needs. One of the most important things to remember when planning your cruise is to gather as much information as you can before you reach into your wallet and dish out money. Having the right information beforehand will prevent problems from occurring and eliminate unpleasant surprises once you arrive onboard the ship.

Cruise ships are often referred to as "floating resorts" or "floating hotels," since your life is centered on the vessel for the duration of the cruise. Thus, it's essential that you become familiar with the amenities that a particular ship and cruise line have to offer. You won't want to be booked on a cruise with a family-oriented theme if you are single and looking to party hearty. If you hate sunny, hot weather, you may be happier cruising in Alaska or Canada than in the Caribbean. And if you don't like crowds or glitz, a freighter that accommodates only twelve passengers may please you more than a huge, modern cruise ship that draws a couple of thousand.

Doing Your Homework

Think of preparing for your cruise as if you were preparing for a test at school. You can do just enough work to make a passing grade, or you can do a more thorough research job and score an A+—which translates into an excellent vacation! Even if you're a frequent cruiser, there are always new things to learn.

Begin by asking yourself the following questions:

Are you planning a cruise because this is a vacation you really want to do or has someone talked you into joining them?

Is this trip "just a vacation" or will you be traveling to a much-anticipated destination?

How much money are you comfortable spending?

Have you anticipated "onboard" costs such as alcoholic drinks, casino spending, souvenirs, tips, and shore excursions?

Have you factored in pretrip expenses such as the cost of getting to the airport, hotel costs for lodging prior to your cruise, gasoline if you are driving to the port, and any necessary visas or inoculations?

Don't forget some destinations charge a tax, such as the state of Hawaii, which adds a .04% tax to your cruise price for ships making round-trips from the state. Always check to make sure that the cruise price you are quoted includes all the taxes and port charges.

Check the cruise-line Web sites to determine the cost of the shore excursions you would like to purchase, and factor those into your budget.

Add a cushion for any unexpected medical costs. The average cost for a visit to the ship's doctor for a cold or tummy virus is about $100.

A passport is needed for many destinations, so remember to give yourself plenty of time to get or renew a passport.

Trip and cancellation insurance is another item to factor into your costs. If you travel frequently, ask the insurance agent to quote you for a yearlong rate rather than just the length of your cruise. Who knows? After one cruise you may be ready to go again in no time at all!

Now, with a reasonable budget in mind, is the time to start looking at cruise brochures and talking to agents.

The best sources of information about cruising are cruise agents, cruise-loving friends and family, travel books and magazines, and the Internet. Ask questions and keep notes. First-time cruisers have hundreds of questions pertaining to their cruise. A good place to begin your information quest is on the Internet. Try www.cruisecritic.com or www.cruisereviews.com. Both are filled with information from cruise passengers.

There are many cruise Web sites that offer cruise pricing. To avoid becoming overwhelmed with all that's out there in Cyberland, start with www.cruisegroups.com. Ten of the top cruise Web sites are located under one domain name. Each Web site offers different services to people from all walks of life. Or go directly to each individual cruise site and study their approach. Do they talk about cocktail parties or pub nights? Adventures ashore or lots of culture onboard?

Many of the large Internet travel companies are eager to provide cruise prices and make your reservation, but they are not always available to assist if you encounter a problem. If personal service is a priority, deal with a local agent. Of course, it won't hurt to let them know what a terrific deal you found on a Web site. Many agencies will try hard to match that price.

You can obtain a cruise refund, perhaps hundreds of dollars, simply by granting www.cruiserebate.com permission to take over your booking. For anyone who has made cruise reservations directly with the cruise line or onboard a cruise ship, this Web site is highly recommended as a great way to save even more money.

Be aware that not all Web sites are secure. Before you pay for your cruise using your credit card, make sure the company confirms that its Web site is secure and no hackers are able to retrieve your credit card number.

Cruise sale prices that appear in the travel section of a Sunday newspaper are usually not the actual final price. Read the small print at the bottom of the page and be sure the price includes port charges, accommodations, all taxes, and the new "fuel surcharge." Every time you see an increase at the pump, you can count on it being reflected in a higher cruise price.

If you have made your air arrangements to and from the ship through the cruise line, ask your cruise agent to contact the line about a schedule that suits your needs. This usually costs $50 per person and there may be some additional costs from the airline.

Most shore excursions can be booked in advance through the cruise line's Web site. Obtain your reservation or booking number from your cruise agent to use when you confirm your tours.

Where to Go

Where is the best place to cruise? Cruise anywhere, anytime, anyplace! Your worst day on a cruise ship is better than your best day at work!

Cruise passengers are becoming more adventurous about exploring Planet Earth. Now that more and more people are choosing cruise vacations than ever before, new and exciting ports of call such as the Baltic Sea, Canary

Islands, Red Sea, Indian Ocean, Southeast Asia, Amazon River, the South Seas, and even Antarctica are quickly becoming popular cruises. Who would have thought even twenty years ago that you could explore so many remote areas of the world in comfort and luxury, and at such affordable prices?

Check with your local library or bookstore for general information and the history of the ports of call your ship will be visiting. You will have a better understanding and appreciation of each locale when the ship docks and you begin exploring.

~~~~~

The people you meet in the different ports of call are one of the things that you will remember most about your vacation.

~~~~~

A cruise that stops at more ports of call does not necessarily mean a better cruise. Keep in mind that an endless round of ports can become tedious. And many passengers enjoy being at sea as much as, if not more than, being on land.

~~~~~

Unless you have been on a number of cruises and proved to have exceptional stamina, look for a cruise itinerary that is not too demanding, especially if you are not able to walk around easily.

Cruise Tips for Any Destination

Cruises come in all shapes and sizes and can last two, three, four, five, seven, eight, ten, twelve, or fourteen days on all kinds of vessels, large and small. Sometimes a cruise line offers a better cruise value on a seven-day itinerary than on a four-day. Have your cruise agent find you the best value before you make your deposit.

Find out ahead of time if your cruise ship stops in port on a Sunday or local holiday. In some cases the shops and attractions will be closed and there will be nothing to do in the town, so you might want to book a shore excursion on that day.

To enhance your time in each port of call, do research before you go. Purchase a guidebook, search the Web, or contact the tourist boards of each place your ship is docking.

United States Customs currently allows $400 worth of goods per person to be brought back into the country duty-free. Anything over that allotment will be assessed a charge.

Don't think that if you make a large purchase and have the goods shipped home, you can avoid a Customs penalty. The arm of the Customs and duties laws reaches very long distances, especially if you have used a credit card.

Traveler's checks are rarely used much anymore. In fact, they've become more of a burden than a dependable payment method. ATM machines are located on nearly all ships and in the ports of call. You should consider using your credit card for nearly all your purchases.

A word about ATMs onboard and ashore: The access fee can be very steep, sometimes $5 or more.

Call your credit card company before you leave home and let them know you are going to be on vacation. Sometimes credit card companies put a stop on purchases if there is a sudden burst of charges from a location other than your usual area.

The food is exotic and savory in many of the local restaurants in port. Be sure you've packed something to take should any irregularities occur an hour or so after you eat.

When you leave the ship for a non-ship organized activity, make certain to bring with you the ship's daily program listing the very important name and phone number of the local port agent.

If you miss the ship and it sails to the next island without you, contact the cruise line's port agent for assistance. They can help you with transportation to your next port of call. Catching up with the ship will, of course, be at your expense.

Drink bottled water in all the ports of call, no matter what you've heard about it being fine to drink. Drinking water onboard is heavily chlorinated but safe to drink unless advised otherwise.

Caribbean Cruise Tips
(Including the Bahamas and Bermuda)

The Caribbean is to North Americans as the Mediterranean is to Europeans. It's an exciting cruise vacation destination that's close and fun and offers many things to many passengers. Who can resist sailing onboard a cruise ship in 85-degree (Fahrenheit; 29 degrees Celsius) weather in the middle of winter, while enjoying an array of sightseeing and historic attractions? Whether you're snorkeling with the stingrays in the Grand Cayman, looking at the stalagmites inside a cave in Barbados, or simply basking nude in the sun on a beach in St. Martin/St. Maarten, your Caribbean cruise will offer all kinds of exciting things to do and see.

Cruise ships in the Caribbean are designed to provide a variety of options to singles, families, gays and lesbians, seniors, honeymooners, and anyone else looking for an exciting vacation that's relaxing and fun. From rock-climbing walls and sundecks permitting topless sunbathing to state-of-the-art health clubs and private dining rooms, cruise ships in the Caribbean offer it all.

Although not technically in the Caribbean Sea, both Bermuda and the Bahamas are favorite cruise destinations, particularly for travelers from the Northeast. Why? In most cases you can simply drive to your port of embarkation and in no time at all be sailing away to pink beaches and British accents. Here are just a few tips for getting the most out of your Caribbean/Bermuda/Bahamas cruise.

Cruise ships that sail to the Caribbean can originate from one of many U.S. cities: Fort Lauderdale, Miami, Tampa, New

Orleans, Galveston, Baltimore, Philadelphia, and New York City, to name a few. Have your cruise agent price the different locations in the event the cruise line offers a "resident" or "senior" rate.

~~~~~~~~~

Bermuda cruises are different from other cruises because you generally depart from a more northerly East Coast city, such as New York, Boston, or Philadelphia, and because your destination is such an integral part of your cruise. Your ship remains docked there for several days or perhaps moves from one port, Hamilton, to another, St. Georges. However, just because this is a single-destination cruise, you won't lack for things to do. The pink beaches of Bermuda are deservedly world famous and the shopping is fabulous.

~~~~~~~~~

Bermuda is a favorite destination of honeymooners, bridge fanatics, and those who enjoy an island with a very British character.

~~~~~~~~~

Tourist season in the Caribbean for "land" vacationers is from mid-December to mid-April. If you want to cruise when it's less crowded in the ports, opt to cruise from mid-April to mid-December.

~~~~~~~~~

Cruises to the Bahamas are a favorite of those who live in the southern United States because they, too, are so easily accessible. Departing from Port Canaveral, Ft. Lauderdale, and Miami, it takes almost no time at all to sail to the Bahamian islands.

If you are not sure if cruising is for you, these short three- or four-day cruises are a terrific way to try out the at-sea experience.

The newest and largest cruise ships in the world sail in the Caribbean, primarily because of their size and also because the Caribbean is such a popular destination. The larger the ship, the more options there are for groups traveling together. However, keep in mind that the larger the ship, the longer the lines—lines for embarkation, disembarkation, buffets, shore excursions, and tenders.

Back-to-back cruises, alternating the eastern and western Caribbean itineraries, are a wonderful way to relax and enjoy a longer cruise. Have your cruise agent negotiate a good cruise fare. Be sure your cabin location is confirmed in writing and that you are allowed to stay in the same stateroom for both cruises.

No vaccinations are required to sail on a Caribbean cruise. Savvy travelers recognize that the vaccination for hepatitis A and hepatitis B, along with the recent arrival of an oral vaccine that helps prevent traveler's diarrhea, are an excellent idea.

Because cruise ships stop in many remote ports in the Caribbean, federal authorities are always looking for drug traffick-

Ten Great Caribbean Shore Excursions
by Ann Burgess

1. Snorkeling with the stingrays at Stingray City on Grand Cayman Island
2. Climbing the Dunn's River Waterfall in Jamaica
3. Exploring Nelson's Dockyard in Antigua, followed by a rum-punch cruise
4. Shopping for jewelry in St. Thomas or St. Maarten
5. Exploring the Harrison Caves in Barbados
6. Sunbathing nude on the island of St. Martin/St. Maarten
7. Scuba diving the wreck of the *Rhone* in the British Virgin Islands
8. Hiking the El Yunque Rainforest in Puerto Rico
9. Kayaking the Panama Canal from Colon to Sol Melina
10. Visiting the pyramids at Chichen-Itza on the Yucatan Peninsula in Mexico

ing. Guard dogs are frequently brought onboard the ship to sniff out the drug dealers. Do not even think about acquiring illegal drugs while on a cruise.

Hurricane season in the Caribbean is June through November, with most activity occurring during the months of September and October, but don't let that scare you from booking a cruise during this time of year. Cruise lines offer incredible rates on these cruises and the captains of the ships have advance notice to avoid any problems with the weather.

The Caribbean is the number-one cruise destination for families during the summer months and holidays. If you don't want to sail on a cruise ship buzzing with children, opt for an alternative date to cruise.

There is a tendency to overpack for most cruises, especially a Caribbean cruise. Realistically, you are going to be in shorts, a swimsuit, T-shirts, tennis shoes, and sandals most of the time. It's very casual during the daytime. For evening attire, have your cruise agent suggest some options so you don't get too carried away with your packing.

Even though a Caribbean cruise provides an opportunity to enjoy warm weather, pack a sweater. Sometimes the lounges and public rooms on the ship have the air-conditioning set too cold, and you may need some sort of cover-up.

When you are shopping in the Caribbean and you hear that the port is "duty-free," this means no taxes are added to any of your purchases.

Smoke your Cuban cigars on the deck of the ship under the stars. But do not try to bring them home.

U.S. currency is widely accepted throughout the Caribbean. It is always a good idea, however, to have at least $20 in single dollar bills each time you visit a new port in the event the people you are dealing with cannot make change. They also come in handy for tipping taxi drivers, tour guides, and others who provide service while you are ashore.

~~~~~~

Be out on the open decks as the ship pulls in and out of port. Quite often the cruise lines have hired local dancers or calypso bands to play Caribbean music as part of their welcome and farewell.

~~~~~~

Some Caribbean cruises include the Panama Canal in their itinerary. The morning the ship goes through the canal, be sure you are on the top deck toward the front. This is the best place to view how the canal operates. Don't forget to be gracious and generous and share the view with your fellow passengers.

~~~~~~

Taxi drivers on many Caribbean islands negotiate prices. Be sure both you and the taxi driver are clear on the rate before you start. If you are taking a taxi to a particular beach, negotiate the price and the time the taxi driver will return to bring you back to the ship. Pay the taxi driver only upon returning to the ship. This ensures that the taxi driver will come back to pick you up. Otherwise, you may be stranded on a beach with no transportation.

~~~~~~

If you are planning to take an interisland ferry to visit a neighboring island, allow plenty of time to return to the ship. If the ferry is delayed or has mechanical problems, have a backup plan to get you to the ship before it sails.

The island of St. Maarten/St. Martin offers a Dutch side and a French side. If you decide to visit Orient Beach, the nude beach, plan on taking your clothes off. The locals will ask you to leave if you're there just to gawk or take photographs.

If your cruise originates in San Juan, Puerto Rico, fly there a day or so before your cruise begins. You may have some time to stroll the cobblestone streets and explore the forts in Old San Juan or take a quick trip to the rain forest (or maybe even recapture any luggage the airline might have misplaced). More importantly, planning to arrive early gives you a cushion of time in case of flight delays or cancellations.

Use your walkie-talkies and cell phones with discretion. Not everyone is interested in your plans!

St. Thomas offers all kinds of jewelry shops. You can negotiate the best deal if you play one against the other. Suddenly that 5 percent discount they first offered you turns into a 25 percent discount just because you mentioned you were interested in their competitor's jewelry. This basically applies to all purchases.

One of the best souvenirs you can bring back from a cruise in the Caribbean is rum cake. These cakes come in all sizes and prices and are vacuum-sealed so they will pass through U.S. Customs. You can find them in many ports of call and often on the ship as well.

Certain animal items such as tortoise shells are not allowed into the United States. They will be confiscated by Customs authorities and you can expect to receive a hefty fine.

Scuba divers will have a great experience in many Caribbean ports. If you're planning to dive, be sure to bring your scuba certification and dive log. You will not be allowed to rent dive equipment if you forget your documents.

If you have never snorkeled, or even if you have, don't pass up this opportunity. It will be one of the most memorable experiences of your cruise. An inexpensive, disposable camera is a good way to capture your moments under the sea.

The Caribbean sun and clouds can be deceiving. Always wear some kind of sunblock, even if you think you won't burn. It's when you don't think you'll get zapped that you do!

Humidity is high in the Caribbean during the summer months. If the lens of your video camera begins to fog when you walk outside from an air-conditioned room on the ship, wait fifteen minutes or so to allow the camera time to defog.

Late-seating dining is usually the first to be wait-listed when cruising in the Caribbean. If this is important to you, have your cruise agent confirm your dinner reservations as soon as possible.

If you need to call home, wait until the ship arrives in one of the U.S. Virgin Islands. The telephones are just like those at home, and it will be much easier and less expensive to call from there. Check with your cell-phone provider to see if coverage is available in these areas. And remember, not everyone on deck wants to listen to your conversation.

Alaska Cruise Tips

An Alaska cruise is usually the next step up after a Caribbean cruise. You've got your sea legs and you're ready to take on the wilderness, provided you won't be too far from a five-course meal or nightly entertainment. That's the true beauty of an Alaska cruise—all that wilderness from the comfort of your deck chair. Humpback whales, orcas, otters, and glaciers can all be viewed from the privacy of your very own balcony. Just don't expect them to appear on cue.

Alaska cruises can originate from many destinations along the West Coast including Vancouver, Seattle, and San Francisco. Most ships that depart from Vancouver will travel the very snug Inside Passage (between British Columbia's mainland and Vancouver Island), a very scenic route. If you depart from Seattle or San Francisco, most likely you will travel along the west coast of Vancouver Island on your route to Alaska.

The options available for cruising in Alaska range from small expedition ships to large ocean liners. It might be wise to look into all the options before you make a final decision. Normally, the smaller the ship, the more expensive the Alaska cruise.

~~~~~~

Ten Great Shore Excursions in Alaska
by Ann Burgess

1. A whale-watching or wildlife tour from Juneau, Ketchikan, Sitka, or Skagway
2. Saxman Village in Ketchikan for totem poles and Tlingit culture
3. Deep-sea or salmon fishing in Ketchikan or Juneau
4. A glacier excursion in Prince William Sound
5. White Pass and Yukon Train from Skagway
6. Flight-seeing the Mendenhall Glacier while in Juneau
7. Panning for gold in Juneau or Skagway
8. Bear watching on Kodiak Island
9. Eagle watching in Haines at the Chilkat Eagle Preserve
10. Taking a helicopter to a glacier and staging a snowball fight in July

When you are selecting an outside cabin for your Alaska cruise and your ship is sailing northbound, have your cruise agent choose a cabin on the starboard (right) side of the ship and vice versa for southbound cruises. This will provide better scenery for the entire cruise.

The type of ship you choose is important to the success of your Alaska cruise. Unless your cruise agent is experienced with Alaska cruising, you may end up with a ship and cruise line that are not providing the type of cruise that best suits your needs. Do your homework and don't settle for just a regular travel agent's advice.

The smaller cruise ships in Alaska may not provide the same level of medical assistance that the larger ocean liners provide. If you require special medical assistance or if you like the idea of a full hospital facility onboard your ship, opt for the larger, newer vessels instead of the smaller ships.

Because Alaska is so different from any other cruise destination and the scenery so spectacular, it's worth upgrading your cabin to a balcony or, at the very least, a window. You'll have no regrets about paying the extra money.

If you are looking at an Alaska brochure from the cruise lines, don't be scared by the list prices. Cruise agents and Internet companies receive all kinds of great deals, so see what prices they can offer you.

Packing for your Alaska cruise is unlike packing for any other cruise. Because the weather is unpredictable, you have to pack for cold, warm, and rainy weather. Layering your clothing is the best way to avoid overpacking.

Essentials to pack for your Alaska cruise are a lightweight raincoat, umbrella, binoculars, backpack, sweater, hat, gloves or mittens, scarf, and comfortable shoes.

Pack a swimsuit even on an Alaska cruise. The temperature can sometimes reach 80 degrees Fahrenheit (27 degrees Celsius) during the summer months. You may even be tempted to swim in the swimming pool or relax in the Jacuzzi.

Whether you start your cruise in Anchorage, Vancouver, Fairbanks, or Seattle, and you need to fly to your port of embarkation, make arrangements to arrive a day prior to your cruise. This will give you an opportunity to see that city and retrieve any lost luggage in the event the airline loses a piece.

Vancouver is one of the best cities in the world, offering an assortment of things to do. Visit Gastown, Stanley Park, Granville Island, Queen Elizabeth Gardens, and Chinatown. Robson Street offers exquisite shopping and a wide variety of restaurants.

Seattle is not only a contemporary city, but there are some terrific tours to participate in as well. Try a day trip to Mount Rainier, a boat ride through the Hiram Chittenden Locks, the Space Needle, or a city tour with Gray Line Tours.

Southeastern Alaska, where most of the cruise ships sail, is along the edges of a rain forest, so be prepared for rain every day of your Alaska cruise, no matter what month you go. If there is a day it doesn't rain, consider it a gift from god.

Summer months are the best time to see wildlife in Alaska. The humpback whales have returned from the Hawaiian Islands, seals and otters pup in late June, and migrating birds are most abundant during June, July, and August.

What is the best side of the ship for viewing wildlife? The outside! Whales can be to port or starboard, eagles almost everywhere, and glaciers, well, they move so slowly that you have plenty of time to change your position.

Summer months are the most expensive time to cruise in Alaska because of the abundance of wildlife and the pre-sumption of better weather. If you're flexible and can sail in mid-May or mid-September, you may find a much better deal for your cruise.

The difference between an Alaska cruise and an Alaska cruise tour is that a cruise tour includes a land package in Denali

Park. If you opt for the tour, plan on spending at least $1,000 more per person for your package.

~~~~~~~

If you are interested only in a seven-day cruise and not the Denali land tour and you want to save money on airfare, book an Alaska cruise that originates and ends in the same port of call.

~~~~~~~

If you want to add a Denali Park land package onto your cruise and you don't want to pay the high prices the cruise lines charge, contact www.alaskatravel.com/denali-park/tours.html or www.nationalparkreservations.com/denali-national-park-tour.htm for more information.

~~~~~~~

Another option for your Alaska cruise is to include the Canadian Rockies before or after your cruise. This includes traveling into the Canadian Rocky Mountains to Calgary, Banff, and Jasper. The scenery is spectacular and different from Alaska.

~~~~~~~

Early morning and early evening are the best times to spot wildlife as this is when birds and animals are most active. Have your coffee with the orcas and eagles out on deck!

~~~~~~~

When the ship sails into a glacial area such as Glacier Bay, Tracy Arm, or Hubbard Glacier, be sure to be out on deck. Harbor seals often can be seen relaxing on ice floes called "bergy bits" that have calved (broken off) from a glacier.

It's easy to spot bald eagles on your Alaska cruise. Look for something resembling a white golf ball in the trees—this will be the crown of the bald eagle—then get a closer look with your binoculars.

Humpbacks, dolphins, and orcas (also called killer whales) can be found almost anywhere in southeast Alaska. Some traditional viewing areas are Snow Pass, north of Ketchikan, and the entrance to Glacier Bay.

The best way to see any wildlife from the ship is to grab a deckchair, get a deck steward to bring you a "steamer rug" (blanket), wrap your hands around a mug of something warm, and wait. Allow your eyes to adjust to the light conditions and the wave patterns. You will be amazed at the things you will see. Jumping salmon, waterbirds such as surf scoters and murrelets, and yes, whales.

When cruising through the Inside Passage, cruise lines hire both naturalist guest speakers and park rangers who narrate the sights over the PA system out on the open decks. Be sure you are outside and available to walk to either side of the ship when they spot some wildlife.

When you see the glaciers for the first time, it's likely your breath will be taken away. It truly is a sight you won't soon forget. Don't get too involved in videotaping it or you may miss everything else around you. The ship may sell videos of the glaciers, so you can still take home a good souvenir.

One of the best occasions for a photograph is the day the ship sails into a glacial area. If you are cruising with a group, arrange a meeting with the ship's photographer outside on the deck for that magic Kodak moment.

If it's raining on the day your ship sails into a glacial area and you don't want to stand outside with your umbrella, the other good places to watch are from the covered promenade deck or in a lounge that has a lot of windows. Otherwise, a comfortable seat next to the window in the upstairs buffet restaurant will do just fine.

Many Alaska shore excursions sell out before the ship even sails because passengers have booked them ahead of time on the Internet. If there are some shore excursions you don't want to miss, make your reservations in advance. Your cruise agent can assist you with this.

Sportfishing is available in Juneau and Ketchikan, usually on a five-hour tour. This excursion can be booked through the cruise line or directly with some of the fishermen in port. The price includes poles, bait, boat, guide, and fishing license.

When exploring Anchorage, the place to begin is the Log Cabin Visitor Information Center (Fourth Avenue and F Street; 907-274-3531; www.anchorage.net). Here you can receive information about restaurants, art galleries, museums, and events happening around the city.

If you participate in a Salmon Bake tour, where you can enjoy the scenery and sample Alaska specialties, be sure to ask if the dining is indoors or outdoors. If you eat outdoors, Alaska's unofficial state "bird," the mosquito, might be a problem unless you're wearing some kind of repellent. Don't forget to pack some.

Skagway is the gateway to the Klondike goldfield. Before you begin walking around town, make a stop in the visitor center and watch a short film about its history. It will give you a better appreciation of the town.

You can get great shopping bargains toward the end of the tourist or cruising season. By mid-September in Alaska, you might get 50 to 75 percent off.

The U.S. Customs authorities and Canadian authorities have strict regulations that state no arts and crafts objects made from body parts of animals (walrus tusks, scrimshaw, or whale bones for instance) are allowed to enter the country.

Whenever you are hiking through the woods on your own, be sure to carry a bell, or talk or sing loudly as you walk. It might seem a little odd, but bears will run away if they hear you approaching. Bears will attack when they feel threatened or are taken by surprise.

You might consider reading a few books or watching a few movies about Alaska before you sail. It makes the experience more fulfilling. James Michener's *Alaska* provides an in-depth, but highly readable outline of the perils and promises the great land presented to nomads and empire builders seeking fortune in the far north. The poems of Robert Service, a bank clerk during the Gold Rush of 1898, paint a memorable picture of the era. The classic movie *North to Alaska* is a rollicking tale of the era starring John Wayne and Stewart Grainger, although it makes the Gold Rush look like a Sunday in the park. A more realistic look, even though it was intended as a comedy, is Chaplin's *Gold Rush,* a film that gives a whole new meaning to cabin fever and starvation (faced by the miners).

Hawaii, South Pacific, Australia, and New Zealand Cruise Tips

These days it is possible to sail the Hawaiian Islands anytime of year. Norwegian Cruise Lines has based two ships in the Hawaiian Islands that sail from one isle to another during the course of a week. If you wish to depart from the mainland and sail to Hawaii, you may find fewer options available as Hawaii is usually included as part of a "repositioning" cruise. This means the cruise line is moving the ship from one area to another and will make only one call in the Hawaiian Islands. These cruises generally are available in the late spring and late fall, as the ships are moving from the South Pacific to Alaska or vice versa. There are some cruise lines such as Princess, Celebrity, and Holland America that are currently offering round-trip cruises to Hawaii from Los Angeles and San Diego. However, proposed legislation may prevent these cruises unless they can arrange to stop for at least forty-eight hours in a "foreign" port, meaning somewhere in Mexico.

The allure of the islands in the South Pacific for many is the still untouched quality they have. You won't find wall-to-wall souvenir stores or chain discount-jewelry houses, or even a wide array of shore excursions. These are islands, as the Caribbean was once upon a time, to spend lazing on a beach or gazing in awe at the sheer physical beauty of the setting.

In Australia and New Zealand, you will also find cruising to be different than your traditional experiences. Both of these countries are thriving and modern. If you go expecting the Outback only a few blocks from where your cruise ship docks, you will be disappointed. Once away from the major cities, in places such as the South Island of New Zealand's Milford Sound or Australia's Tasmania, you will discover the more remote regions you seek.

Like in the Caribbean, the sun is strong in Hawaii and the South Pacific. Make sure you bring plenty of sunscreen or sunblock, and a hat. A sunburn can give you a case of the miserables in no time flat.

One distinct difference with cruises in the Hawaiian Islands is that the casino will be closed. In most cases, when the

Ten Great Shore Excursions in Hawaii and the South Pacific
by Ann Burgess

1. Honolulu, Pearl Harbor, and the *Missouri* Battleship Museum
2. A submarine adventure on any island
3. Swimming with the dolphins at Sea Life Park in Honolulu
4. Snorkeling in paradise at Hanauma Bay on Oahu
5. The Big Island of Hawaii and Volcanoes National Park
6. Waimea Canyon on the island of Kauai
7. Papeete, Tahiti, the Gauguin Museum, and Point Venus, made famous by Captain Cook
8. Milford Sound and the Fjords of New Zealand's South Island
9. Watching the penguins come ashore at Phillip Island, south of Melbourne, Australia
10. Climbing the Sydney Harbour Bridge in Sydney, Australia

ship departs from a port, the casino will open shortly thereafter. Not so in Hawaii. Until you leave the Hawaiian Islands, no gambling is allowed. Don't worry: Watching volcanoes fume and waterfalls tumble is far superior to the *ching-ching* sound of the slot machines.

Other than in Hawaii, don't expect to find all of your favorite brands in stores. Selection can be very limited for toiletries, particularly in the more remote islands such as Fiji or Bora-Bora.

In the South Pacific Islands, expect to be greeted with warm smiles and a very hospitable welcome. Unlike the Caribbean or Alaska, there are fewer ships that ply these waters and the arrival of a cruise ship is still a major event on many islands.

Land excursions in the South Pacific are often taken on "buses" that can be rickety jitneys with plenty of character but no back support. Don't expect air-conditioning every time you open a door, and be sure to carry an umbrella with you for unexpected passing showers.

Take water with you. Yes, you will find water ashore, but make sure you bring your own so you don't spend your entire time ashore in quest of hydration.

Expect items to be expensive. Almost everything has to be imported, and with rising fuel costs, prices are soaring ever upward. Newspapers, books, and postcards have all come a long way to be for sale in the South Pacific, and that journey will be reflected in the cost.

Cruises among the South Pacific islands of Tahiti, Rarotonga, Fiji, and others frequently originate in Tahiti and make round-trips around the various islands.

The South Pacific, unlike the Caribbean, is not so inclined towards public nudity on the beaches. The missionaries of the nineteenth century did their job very well.

Pay attention to State Department travel warnings (http:// travel.state.gov). Some areas, such as Fiji, seem to break out in revolution on a fairly regular schedule. Be prepared to be hastily summoned back to your ship.

Cruises to Australia and New Zealand only generally originate in Auckland, New Zealand, or Sydney, Australia, making calls in one country and then heading to the other. It's possible to join a ship in Seattle, Los Angeles, or Honolulu and continue to Australia and New Zealand, but these are usually repositioning cruises (when a ship is moved from one location of passage in the world to another area of passage; often the ships are repositioned seasonally).

Don't forget that your passport will need to be up to date. Many countries and cruise lines insist that your passport be valid for at least another six months after your embarkation date.

There are various regulations for visiting these countries (for instance, you need a visa for Australia and New Zealand). Be sure to ask your travel agent to verify the current requirements for the destinations you will be visiting. In most cases visas can be applied for online at small cost.

Europe Cruise Tips

London, Venice, Rome, Amsterdam, and Copenhagen are just a few of the ports of call that you can experience on a European cruise. Years ago the most popular European cruises were in the Mediterranean Sea centered on the Greek Islands. Today, if a ship can drop anchor, be it on an ocean or river, most likely you'll find a cruise ship calling.

You can find almost every size of ship plying the waters in and around Europe. Petite river boats that carry only 200 or so passengers, small cruise ships holding 700 to 800 passengers, midsize vessels of 1,500 plus passengers, and, of course, the mega-liners carrying at least 2,000. Your choice will be determined by not only where you want to go, but how you wish to cruise. If the Danube is your desire, you will cruise on a very small river ship. The larger ships are found in the major seaports and call at such places as Istanbul, Rome, Amsterdam, Stockholm, and Southampton.

Most European cruises will depart from Athens, for the Greek Islands and Turkey; Venice, for the coast of Italy and Greece; Rome, for the western Mediterranean and the coast of Italy; Barcelona, for the Spanish and northern African coasts; Southampton, for North Sea, Baltic, and Mediterranean cruises; and Amsterdam and Copenhagen, for Baltic cruises.

What can you expect from a European cruise? A taste of many places. The cruise will allow you to sample the flavor of many destinations, just as it does in the Caribbean. Except in

Europe you may be deciding on which countries and cities to revisit, not just islands.

A European cruise is also one of the most cost-effective ways to visit Europe—beginning with the air package you can purchase with your cruise, transportation to and from the ship, and even the day-to-day costs, to simply not having to buy additional meals or expensive hotel rooms.

Shore excursions in Europe, as in most other cruise destinations, are designed to maximize the time you have available onshore. Keeping this in mind, you may want to be careful not to overschedule your days. You don't have to see absolutely everything. Ask yourself this: "Would I visit this museum, cathedral, or monument if it was in the town where I live?"

Where your ship docks in Europe is also quite different from other locations. Ports were places designed for trade and freight, not passengers of luxury ships. Don't be dismayed by the dismal buildings or dicey neighborhood—this is, after all, the docks. Expect a short shuttle-bus ride to the heart of the city, the cost of which will most likely be additional.

European cruises will take you to places you might not expect. To dock in downtown Helsinki or Stockholm, cruise the inside of a fjord in Norway, or sail past the yacht-packed Riviera are delights that cannot be duplicated from land.

Ten Great Europe Shore Excursions
by Ann Burgess

1. Hermitage Museum, St. Petersburg, Russia, one of the world's greatest art collections
2. Stockholm's "Old Town" (Gamla Stan) and Vasa Viking Ship Museum
3. The "Old Town" of Tallinn in Estonia
4. Athens, the Acropolis, and the Parthenon
5. Rome, a sightseeing tour of the "Eternal City" including the Vatican, Coliseum, and Trevi Fountain
6. Istanbul, the Grand Bazaar, and Blue Mosque
7. Amsterdam, a boat ride on the canals, and a visit to the Van Gogh Museum
8. Archaeological ruins of Ephesus in Turkey
9. Oslo's Viking Museum and City Tour
10. Any day trip to a European capital such as Paris, Berlin, or London

What about barges? These are floating hotel rooms and dining rooms that are towed by a motored boat along a river. In general they take only about a dozen passengers and are one of the most expensive of the cruising options. If you want to slowly tour the wine country of France, this is an excellent way to do so.

For the physically challenged, Europe can be challenging. Not every country and city has made all of its streets, transport systems, and buildings wheelchair accessible. You can expect your shore-excursion desk to be up to date on what destinations and sights will be practical for you, but don't expect that everything will be available.

Should you bring your children? Why not? Most cruise lines do have activities for younger passengers. You may even experience a different Europe if you go light on the cathedrals and make time for more child-friendly activities such as amusement parks, planetariums, and playgrounds.

Cruising northern Europe, such as the Baltic Sea or the Norwegian coast, can be a chilly surprise. Dress in layers to accommodate changing weather conditions.

Don't immediately panic if while onshore you see what seems to be your ship departing much earlier than expected. Harbormasters frequently reposition ships depending upon tidal conditions, but always check your watch and give yourself plenty of time to be settled back on the ship before its scheduled departure.

For eastern Mediterranean travel, cruise passengers should be aware of the sensibilities of local residents in more conservative countries. If you wouldn't wear a bathing suit for a walk down the main street of your town, why would you do it in Cairo? When in doubt about what to wear, cover up. Shorts, yes, just not too short. Shoulders should be covered with a sleeve. Expect that when you visit shrines and mosques that you may be asked to wear a head covering.

Be sure to ask your agent or cruise line to verify where you may need a visa. In St. Petersburg, Russia, you do not need a visa if you are participating in shore excursions organized by the ship, but if you are traveling independently, you will need a visa.

Euros are now the most accepted currency in Europe. Some countries, such as Great Britain, are still using their own monetary units. It is best to change small amounts of money so that you don't end up with too much change in too many currencies. The U.S. dollar is still accepted in many places but not quite so readily as in previous years.

Dress conservatively if your excursions involve places of worship. Casual clothing is accepted, but skip the shorts and sleeveless sundresses.

Most of the port cities in Europe are easily walkable, although you may have to take a shuttle from the port area to the downtown or historical districts.

Wheelchair accessibility still has a long way to go in many of the "old" cities. Ask the shore-excursion manager where you may encounter difficulties.

Size Matters!

Like people, cruise ships come in all sorts of shapes and sizes. Some are classy, with sleek lines, while others are somewhat brassy. Some are huge and a bit show-offish, some very romantic and intimate, and others just efficient and functional. A larger ship is not necessarily a better ship—and vice versa. Your personal preferences as to size and other defining characteristics of a ship, such as age, should dictate your choice.

Think of a large ship as a floating resort and a small ship as a floating inn or hotel.

~~~~~~

The smaller the ship, the more intimate the surroundings and personalized the service on the cruise. It is also likely to be more expensive. These types of cruises tend to attract older and more sophisticated travelers.

~~~~~~

Smaller ships provide quick and easy disembarkation when the ship is docked in port, not to mention on the final day of the cruise.

~~~~~~

Generally speaking, the smaller the ship, the more the cruise line has focused on the ports of call and shore-excursion program.

~~~~~~

The promenade deck on a larger cruise ship completely wraps around the ship, whereas the promenade deck on a smaller vessel may wrap around only three sides.

Larger vessels, for the most part, have more people, more noise, and more activities.

The larger cruise ships provide a greater assortment of activities and entertainment for passengers of all ages.

Generally speaking, the larger the ship, the more lavish the production shows, casino, swimming pools, health club and spa, and sunbathing areas.

The larger the ship, the greater the chance that you will be tendered ashore in smaller boats.

Sometimes the size of the ship is less important than the age of the ship. New ships offer the latest technology, with conference rooms and computers that are connected to the Internet, interactive television, enormous playrooms for children, and state-of-the-art health and beauty facilities. The cabins are fresh and more attractive, and the shower stalls are comfortably sized. The public rooms provide more space, and the entire ship is made to accommodate large groups of people. Nearly all the major lounges are wheelchair accessible, and the ships boast more-sophisticated safety systems.

~~~~~

Many older ships have larger cabins with more closet and drawer space. These ships can withstand a storm better than some newer ships because they were constructed with deeper drafts. There are usually more intimate spaces available in the public areas, and there are more classic nautical lines and wood inlays, as opposed to neon lights and water slides.

~~~~~

The maiden voyage of a cruise ship is exciting, but problems are inevitable. Don't expect everything to be perfect. As with all things that are brand-new, it takes some time before the kinks are worked out. Wait a couple of months, then sail.

Types of Cruises

The cruise industry, more than any other segment of the travel industry, boasts a nearly endless variety of options for travelers. When they hear the word cruise, most people immediately think of coastal voyages. But there are also riverboat and river barge trips, round-the-world cruises, tall-sailing-ship cruises, freighter and cargo-ship cruises crossing from one continent to another, and special expedition cruises. While they are all different, each of these specialty cruises offers a great opportunity for vacationing on a ship.

Special educational cruises are available through some cruise lines. How about traveling to the Galápagos with a team of biologists and oceanographers? Or cruising to ports in Greece and Turkey with a group of archaeologists? Not only will you get to visit exotic places, but you will learn a great deal as well.

A cruise through the Panama Canal is not only educational but will also give you the opportunity to cruise in both the Caribbean and Pacific on the same voyage. And you can get a great price if it's a repositioning cruise between the Caribbean and Alaska.

Many cruise ships sail to their own private islands. These are wonderful places to just lie on the beach and relax. Look for this special option in cruise itineraries.

A transatlantic cruise is a seafaring adventure, and one that is quite reasonable in price. (Before undertaking this particular kind of cruise, however, make sure you have your sea legs.) Transatlantic voyages involve five to eight days at sea with no ports of call.

The obvious difference between cruising on a cruise ship and cruising on a river barge is the body of water on which you travel. A barge will cruise down charming narrow waterways and through canals and locks, entering areas of the world that large cruise ships could never reach.

Don't think of a barge cruise as sailing on a tugboat. Many river barges are luxurious floating hotels, complete with elegant china, rich wood paneling, hot tubs, saunas, goose-down beds, and even fireplaces.

If you don't want constant activities, formal nights, or a casino, a cargo ship or freighter can be an interesting option. These ships carry very few passengers and itineraries can change at the drop of an anchor.

Passengers on a cargo ship are more relaxed, more flexible, and usually have more time to cruise.

A world cruise is one of the most prestigious adventures of all. These cruises often last for months, and the cost can easily reach $100,000 per person. The lines that offer world cruises also allow passengers to book just one portion or section of the cruise—a good way to meet fascinating seasoned travelers at a fraction of the time and cost of a true world cruise.

You may enjoy taking a theme cruise—perhaps one with sports celebrities, country-western stars, jazz musicians, or even one that features rock oldies. Contact your cruise agent for a list and the dates of these cruises.

If you are an active person, a cruise onboard a sailing cruise ship may be just the ticket. Even though these ships are engine-powered for the most part, sails are used from time to time and you can join in and lend a hand. These ships typically travel to more-remote places and offer more adventurous shore programs.

The most fascinating and educational trips are the expedition and nature cruises. These provide a hands-on experience with wildlife, the environment, and the sea. The prices for these cruises are higher than for most other types, but they are well worth the investment for those with adventurous spirits.

Details, Details:
Planning Your Cruise

OKAY, YOU HAVE THOUGHT about what part of the world you want to cruise in, the size of ship that appeals to you, and what type of cruise suits your needs and interests. Now it's time to start putting together the details that will form the basis of your wonderful cruise vacation.

The Perfect Cruise Agent

The basic element in a good cruise experience is having a good cruise agent. In planning a cruise, the right agent can save you literally hundreds of dollars, if not thousands. Forget riffling through the Sunday travel section of the newspaper and signing up directly with a cruise line that advertises a tempting bottom line (there are usually many restrictions and hidden costs). You need a cruise expert to arrange the cruise that's right for you.

The perfect cruise agent is one who has been on more than a dozen cruises, one who will not accept the first price offered by a cruise line, one who has sailed with more than one cruise line, and one who provides more information than you ever thought possible.

~~~~~~~~~

There are three basic ways to make your cruise reservations: directly with the cruise line, through a cruise agent, or on the Internet. All three are fine, if you have enough information before you leave on your cruise.

~~~~~~~~~

A frequent cruiser needs only a good cruise price, because previous experience will provide all the answers needed. The cruise line might offer some specials that the Internet companies are not aware of. A cruise agent is available to answer all the questions you might have and take care of any special requests you will need. However you make your reservations, be sure to check out all your options.

~~~~~~~~~

Some cruise lines have sales agents onboard that can book a future cruise for you. Don't worry about offending your current agent: The cruise line will make sure your agent receives proper credit. Onboard sales agents often have the most-up-to-date information on new itineraries and special deals for frequent cruise passengers.

To determine if an agent is qualified to plan your cruise, ask a few pivotal questions: How many cruises have you personally been on? What makes you special as a cruise agent? Why do you feel you can provide a better cruise package than the competition? What cruise lines do you work with on a regular basis, and why? How many years have you been involved in the cruise industry? Do you have an Accredited or Master Cruise Counselor designation from the Cruise Line Industry Association?

Word of mouth is a great way to find a good cruise agent. Ask your friends, family, even business associates if they have any recommendations.

When considering working with a cruise agent, ask her/him for the names of several cruise clients who have used her/his services in the past. If the agent is reluctant to give you this information or makes any excuses, look for another agent.

Your dealings with a cruise agent should be fun—your relationship sets the tone for your vacation. If your personalities don't click early on, it's best to find another agent.

If the cruise agent you have chosen is insistent on one particular cruise line and does not offer any other suggestions, it may be that he receives a higher commission from that cruise line. Ask the agent to give you information about two or three other cruise lines offering the same kind of product and price. If he doesn't seem enthusiastic, consider moving on to another agent who is interested in your needs rather than the commission.

A good cruise agent wants to do everything possible to plan the best cruise vacation for you, so give as much information as you possibly can. Be specific about how much money you are willing to spend, where you want to go, how long you want to travel, whether you want a quiet, relaxing cruise or an active one, and so on. In other words, do your homework before you walk into the cruise agency.

Ask your cruise agent to arrange the details for a special-occasion cruise. A cruise is a terrific place to celebrate a birthday, anniversary, graduation, family reunion, or maybe just the fact that you have enough sense to celebrate life! Cruise lines are happy to accommodate any special requests, within reason.

Cruise lines are very accommodating, especially when it comes to specific dietary needs. No matter if it's a salt-free, low-fat, or vegetarian diet, you should have no problem receiving the dinner you are looking for, provided you make these arrangements beforehand with your cruise agent. Once onboard, don't forget to follow up with the maitre d'.

Good cruise agents are worth their weight in gold. Once you've found one, show your appreciation with compliments, thank-you notes, and referrals.

Qualifications to Look for in an Agent and Agency

The way an agent and agency present themselves is exactly the way they will handle your cruise requests. Does your agent look sloppy and lack energy and details, or is she sharp and tailored, full of energy and a sense of humor? Is the agency cluttered and disorganized, with tatty, sun-bleached cruise-ship displays in the window, or does it look tidy and busy, with happy employees and customers?

Look for the CLIA (Cruise Lines International Association), ASTA (American Society of Travel Agents), NACOA (National Association of Cruise Oriented Agencies), or ARTA (Association of Retail Travel Agents) emblem on the front door or window of the travel agency. This means that it is a legitimate agency.

If a cruise agency in your area is aggressive in its promotions and advertising, chances are it will be just as vigorous in finding you the best deals on your cruise.

Some cruise agencies place advertisements in newspapers or magazines, claiming to be the exclusive representative for a particular cruise line. Don't be fooled by these ads. No cruise line is exclusive to one travel agency.

Selecting Your Cabin

Even if you expect to use your cabin just as a way station—breezing in and out to catch a few z's and to shower—choosing the right one for you is an important part of planning your cruise. Your selection will affect not only the price but also the general tone of your adventure.

~~~

Think small. In fact, think very small. Don't expect your cabin to be as spacious as those pictured in cruise-line brochures. (When they shoot the cabins for brochures, photographers often use wide-angle lenses that make them look larger than they are.)

~~~

View your cabin as you would your bedroom. How big and fancy does it need to be? If the bare essentials of space and amenities will do, ask your cruise agent to look for lower-cost options. If you typically enjoy time spent in your hotel room as much as any other part of a vacation, allocate a larger portion of your budget to a more luxurious cabin.

~~~

Ask your cruise agent to inquire about the drawer space, wardrobe space, and bathroom facilities in the cabin you are thinking of booking. If you know the actual dimensions, you won't be unpleasantly surprised when you get on the ship.

If you book an outside cabin with a window (typically more expensive than an inside cabin), have your cruise agent check the ship layout to make sure that a lifeboat does not block the view—unless, of course, you willingly receive a discount on the cabin.

On many of the newer ships, the cabin size is the same whether you are on the fifth deck or the ninth (excluding the suites, of course). Why pay more for a higher deck?

Beds onboard a ship are called berths. Some berths are side by side, and some are upper and lower. Ask your cruise agent to find out exactly where these berths are located in the cabin. Honeymoon couples and those seeking a little romance will not be too happy if the twin beds are bolted to the floor!

Avoid booking your cabin above or below the disco or above the propellers. There is a considerable amount of noise and vibration in these cabins.

If you can afford it, book a suite with a private veranda. You'll have delicious privacy while lying in the sun, viewing the scenery, and enjoying a private dinner. When booking a private balcony, make sure it is private. On many ships, the balcony cabins are just below some of the main decks and passengers can look down onto your balcony.

～～～

Be aware that if you have a balcony cabin located just below the pool deck or sports deck you may get substantial noise from all the action above, plus the ship's workers cleaning late at night moving deck chairs around. It's recommended to obtain a balcony cabin that has cabins above and below.

～～～

Most cruise ships provide a shower facility, not a bathtub, in a standard cabin.

～～～

When money is no object, you might consider booking the penthouse suite on an upscale cruise line rather than a regular suite on a luxury line. This will give you your own personal cabin steward, butler, maid service, and plenty of luxurious extras.

Discounts and Upgrades

When you are planning your cruise, remember that there are always ways to get a better fare than the first one quoted. Ask your cruise agent to really dig to find the best possible price. More times than not, the agent can obtain a discount or cabin upgrade for you simply by asking the district sales manager of the cruise line for help.

If you're looking for nothing but the lowest cruise fares possible, and you don't need the assistance of a cruise agent, try Web sites such as www.cruisedirectonline.com, www.cruisedeals.com, and www.cruisesonly.com. Provide them with the specifics of what you're looking for and they can usually give you a quote, all within minutes.

If you have cruised in the past with a particular cruise line and are planning to book another cruise with the same company, ask your cruise agent to inquire about a free category upgrade for your next cruise. Cruise lines may accommodate such requests, providing the ship has available cabin space.

Cruise lines frequently offer two-for-one deals. If you come across any bargain rates—written or oral—ask your cruise agent to investigate. These deals are restricted to certain dates and ships, and a two-for-one rate is quoted from the prices listed in the brochure. Quite often these rates are more than what a last-minute discount would be.

Many cruise lines offer a discount for a third or fourth person traveling in your party, provided you all stay in the same cabin.

Cruise for free! Organize a group of sixteen people or more, and you can cruise for free. Your cruise agent can give you more information.

Cruise lines offer substantial discounts on their repositioning cruises—when a cruise ship is being moved, or repositioned, from one area of the world to another. The most common months for this are April and October.

Some cruise lines now offer the opportunity to charge your entire cruise vacation to a credit card provided by the cruise line. You are then allowed two to three years to pay for the entire vacation. Be careful, however, as the interest rates for these cards can be sky-high and you may end up paying significantly more for your cruise.

Sometimes cruise lines offer promotional rates to single cruisers if they book at the last minute. Your cruise agent can help you with this.

Certain cruise lines also offer a share-a-cabin program to single cruisers. If you agree to share a cabin with a person of the same gender, nonsmoker or smoker, then you may be offered the double-occupancy rate. If the cruise line is unable to find a suitable share, you could end up with a cabin to yourself at a great rate. Or you could find a great future travel companion. The worst-case scenario is that you won't be truly compatible and will end up spending a lot of time outside of your cabin.

If you book your cruise a year in advance, you could receive a substantial discount. You will also be one of the first passengers considered if and when the ship offers any free cabin upgrades.

A back-to-back cruise is two consecutive cruises combined into one long one. Some cruise lines offer a substantial discount if you book this kind of trip. Back-to-back cruises are fun and provide wonderful prices if you have the time; however, there is no guarantee you will remain in the same cabin for both cruises. Your cruise agent should confirm this in writing from the cruise line before you leave.

For individuals or groups who are Christians, www.onholy waters.com is the cruise Web site worth checking out. This entire company is staffed by Christians who all provide great customer service in addition to offering back to your church a percentage of the commission from your cruise.

If the cruise line terminates your cruise midway through the voyage due to mechanical problems, health concerns, or the like, it may be responsible for providing you with up to a full refund or a credit towards another cruise. In most cases, the refund will be made through your cruise agent.

Booking Your Cruise

Booking the cruise is the first big step to your adventure. Make sure you have all the information beforehand—in writing—so that you feel comfortable paying your deposit.

Give your cruise agent ample time to find the best price and the best ship for you. It takes a little extra effort to design a good cruise package.

If you are booking your cruise through an Internet company, be sure you have the name of the agent who will be handling your cruise and his telephone number in the event you have to call him because you're having problems through the Web site.

If possible, book a one- or two-day prepackage before your cruise. That way you have a couple days to enjoy your port of embarkation before departure. It also allows time for any lost luggage to catch up with you or some extra time to cope with flight delays or cancellations.

Read all of the fine print in the "terms" portion of the cruise ticket before paying for your cruise. If there is anything you do not understand, have your cruise agent explain it to you until it all makes sense.

When a family is traveling together and two or three cabins are reserved, the name of at least one adult family member must be on each cabin. Once you arrive onboard the ship, little is said if you change the configuration to suit your family's needs. But if your teenagers behave outrageously and annoy passengers in adjoining cabins, you may have some explaining to do.

If possible, pay for your cruise with a credit card. If any problems arise, the credit card company can assist in sorting out the situation.

Even if you have already placed your cruise deposit with a cruise agent, if a better deal comes along with another company for the exact same cruise, you can cancel your reservation with the original agent. But first make sure you are not under any penalty restrictions and that you have investigated the situation thoroughly. Contact www.cruiserebate.com for more information.

Port charges are added to the cost of the cruise and will be reflected in your cruise ticket. These typically are about $50 to $200 per person, depending on the itinerary.

If a two-category cabin upgrade is offered when you are booking your cruise, it may not be a better location than the original category. A midship cabin in a lower cabin category is preferable to a higher-category cabin toward the front of the ship or above a noisy lounge.

If you book your own air transportation to the ship, be sure not to book a return flight before 12:30 p.m. If the disembarkation process is slow or delayed, you may miss your flight, and the cruise line will not be responsible for helping you reschedule another.

Air-sea packages (which means you've purchased your air tickets through the cruise line) usually provide passengers free transfers to and from the ship.

To Insure or Not to Insure?

Pay the extra money for travel insurance, no matter what your age. Life is full of surprises, and sometimes people simply must postpone their vacation. It is well worth the relatively small insurance fee to guarantee a refund in such cases.

Most cruise lines offer insurance at a high rate and do not cover lost luggage, missed cruise connections, or travel delays.

Some cruise lines offer insurance and promise to give you compensation no matter what reason you use to cancel. Be aware that this could be a future cruise credit with their cruise line and not actual money.

If you decide to cancel your cruise, you will receive a full credit only if you submit your notice in writing no later than sixty days prior to the day the ship departs. During holidays, the notice period may be ninety days.

Some travel-insurance companies have an exclusive family plan in which children 16 years and younger receive full coverage at no additional charge when accompanied by adults who purchase the policy.

You never know what type of medical emergency could occur on your vacation. Buy insurance that covers a medical emergency evacuation from the ship.

On the Road to the
High Seas

THERE'S SOMETHING ABOUT going to sea that makes people feel like they have to be more prepared than when they travel on land (or, for that matter, in the air). In actuality, the steps toward embarking on your cruise are much the same as going on any vacation. That said, however, it is also true that knowing what to expect and being well prepared will make your cruise that much more pleasant.

What to Bring

They say that half the fun of going on a vacation is anticipating and planning it. Preparing your wardrobe and packing for the cruise are part of that fun. The bottom line: Don't get carried away! (Typically, first-time cruisers pack at least twice as many clothes as they need.) One or two bathing suits, a couple of shorts and shirts, a few sets of nice casual wear, and a couple of more dressy outfits should work out just fine. If you feel that you've underpacked (a rare occurrence), you can always pick up something wonderful in the shops onboard the ship or in a port of call.

Don't overpack, don't overpack, don't overpack! Think in terms of essentials. Save room for the stuff you inevitably buy on your trip. Make sure to pack your gear in a suitcase slightly larger than you actually need so that you have room for those souvenirs.

Don't bring the largest suitcase you can find. Suitcases are stored in your room, usually under the bed, during your cruise. You may soon grow to loathe the suitcase you constantly trip over while trying to get dressed.

When taking a seven-day cruise, don't pack more than one piece of luggage and one carry-on bag. Less is better.

Be aware that the airlines are enforcing their carry-on luggage policy, so be sure your cruise agent has provided information regarding the size of your bags. Again, less is always better.

Once you finalize your list of things to take, stick to it. Too often people develop a superb list only to ignore it during the actual packing. Caught up in the heat of the moment, they start tossing things into the suitcase with abandon. Usually these items are never used on the vacation.

A good packing rule to remember when going on a cruise: When in doubt, leave it out!

Bring an attractive cover-up that will carry you elegantly from pool to cabin. In fact, when choosing all of your wardrobe, go for classy rather than gaudy.

Bring a backpack. You can use it as carry-on luggage to and from the ship, and it will be handy both on the ship and on shore excursions.

Pack workout gear if you plan to take advantage of the health-club facilities onboard.

Most cruises provide a mix of casual, informal, and formal evenings. Ask your cruise agent to find out from the cruise line what mix your voyage will offer so you can plan your wardrobe accordingly.

While most cruise ships offer dry cleaning, opt for washable items whenever possible. Who needs the hassle and expense of dry cleaning on vacation?

Many, but not all, cruise lines have passenger washers and dryers available. Some are free and some have a nominal charge.

People often get carried away when it comes to shoes, which take up a lot of luggage space. Try to bring just one pair of walking shoes, one pair of versatile casual shoes, and one pair of dressy shoes. (You certainly know a cruise is not the time to break in a new pair of shoes.)

Give your highest heels a vacation and don't take them on the cruise. It's easy to forget that your floating hotel is actually moving until you find yourself unexpectedly unsteady on your feet.

Pack some moisturized wipes. They will always come in handy, especially when cruising with children and while on shore excursions.

Because of the variety of food offered onboard the ship and in the ports, you may be tempted to try different types of spicy foods for the first time. Pack an antacid, just in case!

A cruise is a great place to show off jewelry, especially on formal evenings, but don't bring anything that you could not bear losing, such as family heirlooms. Costume jewelry is the way to go.

A pareo is a great piece for a woman to bring on a cruise. Essentially a large scarf, a pareo can be wrapped as a skirt, used as a shawl for cool nights on deck, extra shade on a hot beach, or as a blanket under which to snuggle on the airplane ride home.

If you really must bring work with you while on your cruise and you intend to pack your laptop computer, know that most new cruise ships have Internet access in the state-rooms or an Internet cafe. There is a nominal fee and every ship and cruise line is different. Be sure you've packed your laptop in your carry-on bag so it is accessible for airport and pier authorities to check.

Bring a night-light to place in the bathroom or a small flashlight for use in the middle of the night. This will be especially useful for passengers with inside cabins.

If you are traveling with a child who wets the bed, pack a plastic sheet to protect the ship's berth.

Pack a small pair of binoculars, especially if you are cruising to an area where you will be looking at wildlife.

If you wear glasses or contact lenses or take prescription medicine, pack extras in your carry-on bags.

Pack clothing with elastic waistbands. You will feel more comfortable at the end of the cruise, when it is likely you will have gained a pound or two . . . or five!

Don't bring more than a couple of T-shirts. You will probably buy some in the ports of call or in the shops onboard the ship.

Surely you won't forget to bring sunblock or sunscreen!

Toss in a highlighter marker so you can easily mark the activities on the daily program that interest you.

Pack a small first-aid kit to take with you on your shore excursions. This will help if you have a minor injury and do not want to pay for treatment at the medical facility onboard the ship.

Bring insect repellent if mosquitoes or other pesky insects lurk in the ports of call or you will be visiting tropical or boggy destinations. Alaska is notorious for hungry mosquitoes!

If you will be cruising in an area that is warm or hot, pack lightweight, loose-fitting clothes that can be easily washed and dried.

If you will be visiting an area that is cold, pack a warm coat with a lining that can be easily removed.

If you are cruising in an area where the local residents speak a foreign language, pack a small phrase book and memorize some key phrases.

Men will find nylon swim shorts with pockets to be very versatile. They can be used as walking shorts, and they dry quickly.

Pack toiletries, prescriptions, and other things you can't do without, plus a change of clothing, in one of your carry-on bags. In the event your check-in luggage is lost or stolen and does not arrive at the ship, you will have some essentials to keep you fresh for a couple of days.

Traveling as a couple or with a companion? Cross-pack and take an outfit for each other in each other's suitcase. If one bag goes astray, you'll at least have some backup clothing until it arrives.

Pack a copy of your living will. Unfortunately, a cruise vacation is not immune to life-threatening situations.

Bring an umbrella to protect you from rain, snow, or sun.

Pack a hat, pack a hat, pack a hat! A hat with a chin strap is less likely to take off into the wild blue yonder as the ship cruises along at 20 knots per hour. Tilley hats are the mark of a seasoned traveler.

Invest in a good pair of sunglasses. Even in frigid regions, the glare from the sun can be intense onboard.

Even though most cruise ships provide a wake-up service, pack a battery-run alarm clock. (And don't forget extra batteries.)

Although every effort is made to keep you comfortable inside the ship, the air-conditioning can get too cool in some of the public lounges. Pack a sweater or jacket, preferably versatile enough in style to carry you from day to night.

When flying from a very cold climate to a very warm point of embarkation, pack your coat in your luggage just before you check it in with the airline agent.

It needs to be said again: Don't overpack!

How to Pack

Packing well may be an art form, but there's nothing mysterious about it. These tips will help you organize your belongings to minimize clutter and wrinkling and to allow for easy "loading" and "off-loading" both before and after your trip.

Pack your liquid toiletry items in sealable plastic bags, and place these bags in another sealed plastic container. This is double protection against damaging your clothing or other items in your suitcase. Also make sure these containers are not filled to the top.

Special toiletries note: Increased airline security regulations limit your carry-on liquids to no more than three ounces in any one bottle, and you are allowed to fill only one one-quart clear plastic bag, so be sure to pack any toiletries in your checked luggage.

Place the heaviest items on the bottom of your suitcase and the lighter items on top.

Protect your clothing from shoe polish by slipping each of your shoes into an old sock or a plastic bag.

Fold shirts and blouses by making the crease below the waistline. This will help prevent wrinkle lines across the areas that show.

Packing light is the best revenge. If you can manage to pack all your belongings into two carry-on bags, you will save time and not risk having your luggage tampered with or lost. It might be wise, however, to have your cruise agent check with the airline to see how many carry-on bags are allowed per passenger.

When you are cruising to a place that will require you to wear a heavy coat, don't pack it, carry it instead. This is also true for boots, heavy sweaters, or anything bulky that will take up a lot of room in your suitcase.

Expandable luggage will prove to be beneficial when you are bringing home the souvenirs you bought during your cruise.

Tie a closed identification tag with your name, cruise line and ship, and address and phone number (preferably those of your business, for security's sake) to the handle of each piece of luggage, including your carry-on bags.

As an additional means of identification, tape the above information to the inside of each piece of luggage in case the outside luggage tag gets torn off. And make sure to add the name of your ship and embarkation port and date.

In most cases, you will be directed or personally escorted to your cabin when you embark on the ship. Your luggage may not arrive for several hours. Don't panic. The crew members on the ship have nearly 4,000 pieces to sort and distribute— it takes time. If the ship is ready to sail and you have not yet received your bags, contact the purser's desk or the house-keeping department to ask for assistance.

In many cases luggage simply gets delivered to the wrong cabin. People with fairly common last names occasionally find their bags end up at the wrong door. If your bag has gone missing, ask the purser to check the passenger list for similar names.

If your luggage gets lost, don't let it ruin your cruise. You can purchase what you need in the onboard gift shop or in the first port of call. (Of course, you already know that irreplace-able items such as prescription medicines and all valuables should be packed in your carry-on bags.)

Do not lock your luggage with small locks or with the com-bination lock that might be on your bags. For security reasons, all bags must be available and easy to open for security inspection.

~~~~~~

If your air transportation is not part of the cruise package, you will have to collect your own luggage in the baggage claim area before transferring to the ship.

~~~~~~

In the event your luggage does not arrive at the ship and the cruise line and airline are unable to find it, you may be entitled to an "onboard credit" for up to $100 in the ship's gift shop. This will allow you to buy toiletries and a few items of clothing to help you get by until the luggage is found. Contact the information desk onboard the ship for assistance. If you purchased the cruise line's travel insurance you may be compensated. Otherwise your insurance claim will be settled on your return home.

~~~~~~

Don't overpack! (Just in case you hadn't gotten the message yet.)

Travel Documents

It's the packet of information that makes your adrenaline flow: your cruise documents. These papers are your ticket to an exciting adventure. Your cruise agent will receive them a couple of weeks before your departure date and will make sure they are in order before mailing them or calling you to pick them up. Keep these documents in a safe place, and once you are onboard the ship, lock them in the safe in your cabin.

Make two photocopies of these documents. Tuck one set into your suitcase or carry-on. Leave the other set with a friend or relative. Be sure to include a copy of your passport and travel insurance, too.

You are not allowed to use a passport as your proof of citizenship if it is due to expire within six months of embarking on your cruise.

Never pack cash, traveler's checks, travel documents, prescription medicine, or other valuable items in your check-in luggage. Keep these with you in a secure carry-on bag.

Proper identification and proof of citizenship are mandatory to board the cruise ship. If you fail to provide this to the cruise line's embarkation staff, you will not, under any circumstances, be allowed to board the ship and no refund will be given to you. A valid passport or certified copy of your birth certificate is needed.

When cruising abroad, ask your cruise agent (at least six months in advance) if you will need a vaccination or medical certificate. Some countries require these, and you do not want to leave such things to the last minute.

Your cruise agent will let you know if you will need a passport to enter any ports of call. Obtaining a passport is easy and relatively inexpensive. Call the United States Passport

Agency to obtain information (its twenty-four-hour phone number is 202-647-0518), or go to www.travel.state.gov. You can also call your local post office for information.

Navigating Air-Sea Transfers

Your house is locked up tight, mail and newspaper delivery has been stopped, and Rover has been left in the neighbor's care. Finally, you're ready to leave on your big adventure!

But before you can begin cruising, you may have to fly to the embarkation point. While it's true that transfers between airports and cruise-line terminals can be tedious, a few tips should help ease the pain.

Connecting flights have a way of making people tired. Opt for nonstop flights to your embarkation port whenever possible, even if it costs a bit more.

If your flight to meet the ship is long, wear casual clothes on the plane. Take off your shoes and put on a thick pair of socks. You'll feel much better and arrive in better spirits.

When cruising during big holidays, arrive at the airport at least three hours before your scheduled flight. Airlines do occasionally overbook, the people who check in first have priority, and latecomers will be bumped.

Have your cruise agent book an early enough flight so that you will not panic about missing the ship. It is advisable to fly a day prior to embarking onto the ship. When you get off the airplane, you will be greeted by a cruise-line representative, either at the gate or in the baggage claim area. The representative will tell you what to do and where to go from there.

If you've purchased a hotel package with the cruise line, ask your cruise agent to confirm that there will be ground transportation from the airport to the hotel and to the ship the following day. Be sure you have transfer coupons for this.

Take special care in transferring your luggage in and out of taxis and hotels, prior to embarking onto the ship. Be sure you have every piece of luggage with you before you leave these places.

If for any reason you happen to miss the ship, contact the cruise line's port agent at the pier. They might be able to help you with a charter boat or tug to get you to your ship. Otherwise, they'll help arrange air transportation to the ship's next port of call. This emergency transportation will be at your expense, however.

For security reasons, passengers are not allowed to bring visitors onboard the ship, even on the day of embarkation.

If you fly to another country to meet the ship, you will be required to collect your luggage and pass through Customs.

At that point you will be instructed by the cruise-line representative on where to proceed.

Embarkation at Last!

Embarkation. Even the sound of the word generates excitement and fun. It's the start of your long-awaited vacation as you walk up the gangway to go onboard the ship. Not only are you embarking onto the ship, you are embarking on a new adventure. Have fun!

Embarkation is a very busy time for the staff and crew members. When checking in at the cruise-ship terminal, have all your cruise documents filled out and ready to hand to the staff. This will help speed up the embarkation process immensely.

~~~~~

Be prepared to stand in lines awaiting check-in and security screening.

~~~~~

If you live near where you will board your ship, don't arrive too early at the dock. Embarkation almost never begins prior to noon. Why? First the ship must disembark all the passengers from the last cruise and clean the ship.

~~~~~

If you are a frequent cruiser and belong to a cruise line's repeat-passenger club, there is usually a separate check-in place for you and everyone in your party. Sometimes these lines are longer because there are so many repeat passengers. Play it by ear.

At check-in you will be issued a cruise card. Do not lose it. This card is your embarkation pass, room key, and onboard credit card all rolled into one.

If you do lose your cruise card, the purser's office onboard the ship can replace it. However, you will need to show identification.

Many cruise lines, on request, will punch a hole in the cruise card and supply you with a lanyard so that you can hang the card around your neck. This is a good idea, especially if you have a habit of misplacing things.

After your cruise documents have been checked in and you're given a cruise card, you will be directed first to security screening and then directed to where you can walk onto the ship. There is usually a photographer standing at the entrance of the ship, ready to snap a picture of you with your windblown hair, faded makeup, wrinkled clothing, and exhausted smile. Don't worry: You can use that photograph as your "before" cruise picture.

If the ship's crew members escort you to your cabin, give them a tip. Just like hotel employees, these ladies and gentlemen are accustomed to receiving a couple of dollars for their service.

~~~~~~

Once you have unpacked your clothing, get a small map of the ship from a crew member if one has not been provided in your cabin, and start exploring.

~~~~~~

As soon as you get onboard, your cruise experience begins in a most welcome way: You most likely will be offered a buffet meal, usually in the cafe on the top deck.

~~~~~~

When your luggage arrives you might find it easier to take turns unpacking, otherwise you may find yourselves bumping into each other due to the compact size of the cabin.

Your Money

Going on a cruise could be the best investment you'll ever make in your life. What you will learn in one week on a cruise is often greater than the education you would get in a semester at college. To get a full return on your investment, know how to handle your money while cruisin'.

~~~~~~

Your onboard cruise card is activated by using a major credit card. This card is also used for identification when you leave and board the ship and sometimes as the key to your stateroom. Don't forget: As with any charge card, this bill has to be paid! If you are on a budget, check your balance frequently to monitor how much you are spending.

Personal checks are rarely accepted onboard a ship, so be sure you have enough cash or credit on your personal credit card to pay for your onboard purchases. Many cruise lines have ATM machines onboard (usually found near the casino) in the event you need extra cash.

Withdraw cash from an ATM when you arrive at your destination in order to get the best exchange rates. Call your credit card company before your trip to find out what exchange rate they are using and if there are any additional fees.

If you are cruising in a foreign country, cruise lines will often arrange for the local bank authorities to exchange currency onboard the ship.

U.S. currency is accepted in many ports of call. Ask the purser's staff for guidance in this area. However, this is rapidly changing with the appearance of the euro and currency fluctuations.

At the end of your cruise, you will receive an itemized statement for all your onboard purchases. After you check it over to make sure everything is correct, your charges will automatically be transferred to the credit card you used to activate your cruise card. You will not have to wait in a long line on the final night to pay your bill.

If you disagree with anything on your bill, discuss it with the purser's staff as soon as you become aware of the discrepancy or on the final night or final morning before disembarkation.

Before making a telephone call from the ship, find out how much it will cost. Sometimes a call may cost up to $15 per minute! Thus, if you need to reach someone at home, wait until the ship docks in port and call from a pay telephone. If you do not have a calling card, in many cases there will be a calling booth nearby where you can buy one.

On some ships and in some ports you can make calls from your own cellular phone. If it's that important for you to be easily accessible by phone, ask your local cellular dealer for details about cell phones with a "roaming" feature.

If you're using a calling card at a pay phone that has a push-button system and you want to make more than one call, don't hang up the telephone when you have completed your call. If you press the # (pound) key after the other party has hung up, you will get another dial tone and won't be charged an additional connection fee.

Settling In

WHILE EACH SHIP and each cruise is unique, there are certain commonalities in the world of cruising. Knowing what to expect onboard from the cruise staff and crew—and knowing what is expected of you and your fellow passengers—will enrich your vacation and the relationships you form onboard.

The Staff and Crew

Most of the staff and crew are genuinely happy to have you onboard the ship, whether it's a luxury liner or a freighter. They are well trained in their jobs, and they are often very interesting people. You'll have no problem making friends among them, and you'll be glad you did.

Just ask! This is one of the best tips in the entire book. You will be amazed at how much the staff and crew of cruise ships are willing to accommodate your needs.

If you have a waiter, busboy, or cabin steward who tells you he may get fired from the cruise line unless you give him an "excellent" rating on the comment cards, report this to the hotel manager onboard the ship. This is not true, and the cruise lines will not tolerate this type of behavior.

Don't ask the captain "Who's drivin' the boat?" if you meet him at the welcome-aboard cocktail party. Spare him—he's heard this line a thousand times.

The ship is your home away from home for a week or so. However, it is home for the crew members and staff for much longer periods. Respect the signs that say crew only. These areas are the only places they have for privacy and to take their minds off work. Think of it this way: Would you want your customers and clients pushing their way into your living room?

The entertainment staff are the fun people onboard the ship, or they should be. Whenever they are involved in an activity or event, you can expect a good time. If they ask for a volunteer to help them out, do it!

At the end of the cruise, you will be asked to fill out a comment card. If you received particularly good service from any staff members, be sure to note their names. This is how many employees on cruise ships get their promotions and raises.

If you are going to criticize something or someone on the comment card, suggest how the problem might be solved. Cruise lines are more receptive to complaints if they are accompanied by a solution.

Is there something wrong or broken in your cabin? First, ask your cabin steward and if the problem is not resolved, write out your complaint, to the captain's attention, and hand it to the purser's desk. This is the fastest way to get a problem resolved.

Get to know the staff early in the cruise. They can give you some wonderful inside information regarding the ports of call, excursions, activities, and so on.

The social hostess or concierge is usually responsible for selecting guests to attend the captain's special cocktail receptions. Talk with either of them if you are interested in attending one of these functions. Sometimes passengers who have experienced an unfortunate mishap on the ship will be invited in order to smooth things over.

It is possible that you are not accustomed to maid service or cabin service as is provided on the ship. Do not let this intimidate you and don't be rude or excessively demanding. These are respectable jobs that require long hours. Be respectful and appreciative of these employees.

There are times when cruise agents have promised that the ship will provide something but, due to circumstances beyond their control, the ship's staff and crew are unable to deliver. For example, the Jacuzzi in your suite may expire halfway through the cruise and the part to fix it won't be available for a week or so. Unless it is a matter of life or death, let it go. Don't allow it to upset you.

Don't ask crew members how much money they earn. Would you like to be queried about your salary?

Tipping Guidelines

One of the questions most often asked about cruising is "What is the proper tipping etiquette?" It is an issue that creates a great deal of anxiety among cruisers, but a few simple guidelines will help you navigate these particular waters. Please follow the suggestions provided here and by your cruise line. What you leave these people as your gratuity for the week is important, not a favor. Be a good tipper.

Some cruise lines include tipping in the price of the cruise fare; others do not. If gratuities are not included in the fare, give what is recommended by the cruise line directly to the individuals who are supposed to receive the tip. Cruise lines will provide special tip envelopes near the end of your cruise.

Some cruise lines now automatically add gratuities to your cruise card bill. This eliminates any concerns you may have regarding tipping. However, if you wish to tip personally, you can ask the Purser's Department to remove the gratuities from your bill.

If the cruise is longer than two weeks, it is customary to tip a portion of the gratuity midway through the voyage and the remainder on the last evening.

The average amount of money for tips for a passenger on a one-week cruise is approximately $10 per day, per person— not a bad deal at all for the fabulous service provided.

Be sure to tip the maitre d' if he or she has arranged something special for you, such as making sure papaya is always available for you at breakfast. If you only see the maitre d' before tipping night, don't bother.

It is not necessary to tip the head of a department, like the cruise director, hotel manager, purser, bar manager, chief cabin steward, or executive chef. These people make great salaries and do not expect any extra compensation for doing their job well. Buy them a drink and toast their professional talent.

Take a moment at the end of your cruise to write thank-you notes to members of the crew and staff who have really made a difference in the success of your vacation. Written words of appreciation are sometimes just as important as the cash tip.

A 15 percent tip is automatically added to the check for most of the drinks and bottles of wine that you order in the lounges. If you have been a regular customer to a particular bartender, however, leave that person some extra money on the last day of the cruise.

What to Do if There Is a Problem

Yes, problems can arise even on a luxurious cruise ship. If they do, take a deep breath—and then get over it! Life is too short to get stressed out about whether someone has cut in front of you while you are standing in line at the midnight buffet or whether you won that imitation-leather key ring at shuffleboard. And if the only problem you run into is the fact that your clothing has inexplicably shrunk by the end of the cruise, consider yourself a contented cruiser!

If there is a problem, gather all the facts before talking with the staff, and don't raise your voice or get hostile. If possible, back up your complaint with documentation or witnesses. If you present yourself as being civilized and level-headed, your complaint will be taken seriously. People who act like hotheads or with hysterics will be viewed more skeptically.

Cruise lines are always anxious to settle disputes with unhappy passengers, provided the complaint is reasonable. The last thing a cruise company wants is bad publicity.

The staff and crew want to do everything possible to see that you have a wonderful cruise. Don't hold in your complaint until the last day and then "let 'em have it" in the comment cards. Doing that only builds some resentment. Speak up early!

Present any complaint to the manager of the department where the problem occurred.

Should you encounter a problem with your cabin—for example, there is excessive noise from the generators, the category of the cabin is not what you paid for, the plumbing is not working correctly—contact the hotel manager immediately and ask to be moved to another cabin. If there are no other cabins available, ask the manager to give you written confirmation acknowledging that these problems do exist. When presented in a fair way, the cruise line may issue you a partial refund. Be sure that your cruise agent follows up on this.

Most types of legal action brought against a cruise line will be heard in a federal court, as all cruise ships operate under maritime law. But this is an ordeal; try to settle any disputes out of court.

If you cannot reach an agreement with a cruise line and feel that your only alternative is to seek legal action, you must act within the deadline specified in your cruise contract. If you don't, you could forfeit your right to any case whatsoever.

If your cruise agent made arrangements with the cruise line's corporate office regarding something special for you onboard the ship, and for some reason it has not come about, talk to the hotel manager's staff. Sometimes inexperienced cruise agents promise things that are impossible for the ship's staff to accommodate. Occasionally, the information from the cruise agent to the office to the ship gets lost. Be patient with the onboard personnel until the problem is solved.

Cruise Etiquette

Can you imagine two 80-year-old ladies fistfighting because they wanted to dance with the same dance host at the same time? Or passengers sitting in their cabin on the last night of the cruise ordering room service so they didn't have to tip their waiter and busboy in the dining room? Although some of the suggestions below may be simple common sense, they serve as a reminder for those who need to brush up on their etiquette.

Don't expect everything to be perfect on your cruise! Brace yourself: It is not going to be perfect, even if you have spent thousands of dollars. You may encounter rough weather, a water pipe may break in your cabin, your dining-table mates might be miserable human beings. No matter what happens, go with the float … um … flow! Have a good cruise attitude!

Laundry can pile up on a cruise, especially if there are children along. Some ships have a laundry facility on each deck. If the ship you are traveling on does not have a laundry facility and you do not want to pay to have your clothes cleaned, fill the sink in your cabin with water and add a dash of shampoo. Hang the clothes to dry on the clothesline above the shower—not draped all over the furniture.

Most cruise ships offer a selection of books in the library. If you check one out during the cruise, be sure to return it before disembarkation. (If you take it home, you may be charged for it.)

Use the right nautical terminology. The ship is called a ship—not a boat. And the port side of the ship is on the left and the starboard side is on the right. (It is easy to remember this because port and left both have four letters.) The front of the ship, or pointy end, is called the bow; the blunt end is the aft.

Elevators will be crowded around mealtimes, before and after the evening shows, and on the morning when passengers are leaving the ship. To help ease the crunch, head for the stairs during those times if possible.

To mail postcards and letters from the ship, take them to the reception desk. The receptionist will have them posted in the next port of call. In most cases, of course, you will have to pay the postage.

There should be complimentary stationery and postcards in your cabin. If you do not find any, contact the information or reception desk.

When leaving your cabin, don't slam the door. Others who are staying in the cabins near yours may be sleeping or resting. Show the same consideration that you would like to receive from them.

The ship is your home for the duration of the cruise, but that doesn't mean normal civilities can be dropped. Be polite and pleasant to those around you.

Keep a grip on yourself. Getting a little tipsy and kicking up your heels on the dance floor is one thing; reeling around knocking over tables in the bar or starting an ugly argument is quite another. If you make a fool or pest of yourself because you have had too much to drink, you'll have to face the witnesses in the morning. You don't want to spend your vacation slinking around the ship, trying to avoid those people.

Be discreet with your money and personal wealth. Nobody really cares, and being ostentatious is in bad taste.

The ship is indeed your home away from home, but it's still a public facility. Don't wander around outside your cabin in a nightie and curlers.

In the same vein, please be modest in your attire. It's not necessary for every person on the ship to become acquainted with your every bulge and curve. Gentlemen please note, there comes a time when the Speedo is no longer appropriate in mixed company.

Don't walk around the inside of the ship in a bathing suit without a cover-up.

If there is a long line to greet the captain at the welcome-aboard cocktail party, relax in one of the lounges until the line tapers off. You can then walk in as an individual and not as part of the herd!

To be asked to dine with the captain is an honor. Don't ever decline.

Don't drape your belongings over the deck chairs to reserve them for later. These chairs are for everyone. Unless you are ready to use them, leave them for someone else.

Don't sit in the front row of an evening show if you are tired and could easily fall asleep after a long day of sightseeing. Others may be distracted by watching your head bob up and down. And the entertainers certainly don't want to look out and see people dozing during their act.

If you are on a cruise where the announcements are translated into three or four different languages, be patient. Sometimes the information concerns safety matters, and it is important that all the passengers understand the procedures.

If you are cruising with another person or group of people, be a good cruise companion. Don't complain or grumble about things. It will not only bring negative energy to your vacation, but you will embarrass the people with you and around you. If there's a problem, handle it quietly and privately with the cruise staff and crew; don't bore your fellow passengers with it.

Give your cabin mate some space so that you don't get on each other's nerves. Agree to participate in a few activities separately, and establish other ground rules before you embark on the cruise.

There is a reason why cruise ships do not sell gum onboard the ship. Parents, make sure your children dispose of their gum in the garbage container and not on or under the furniture.

If you have been trekking through a muddy rain forest during a tour, be considerate and do not track the mud through the ship. Take off your shoes or boots before entering the ship and carry them with you to your cabin. Once you get to your cabin, you can wash them off in the shower.

Sit at least ten rows back from the stage if you are bringing small children to the shows. If they start getting restless and talking, it will be less distracting to the rest of the audience and the performers on stage.

If the sun shines, smile. If it rains, smile and look for the rainbow.

Take a moment to commend any of the staff and crew members you feel are doing a great job. A pat on the back goes a long way.

When traveling with children, make sure they understand that the elevators are not a playground.

Children should not be left to roam the ship unaccompanied. Don't think "We are on a ship, where could they go?" Ships are a different environment with lots of different hazards, including falling overboard.

Make sure your children know how important it is not to run or push people out of the way. Scores of older people, some with walkers and canes, don't respond as quickly as they might, and a fall would devastate their cruise vacation.

Doors leading to the outside of the ship can be especially heavy. Take care that little fingers don't get jammed accidentally when opening and closing these doors.

Cruisin'

SO WHAT IS the secret to having a really great cruise? The passengers who seem to have an absolute blast are those who have a great attitude. These people roll with the punches, are not afraid to participate in the activities, and somehow open their minds and hearts to the cruise adventure. They are nonjudgmental, a quality that allows them to be free spirits onboard the ship. Thus, to make the most of your cruise, follow this motto: Participate, don't anticipate.

Bon Appétit!

One phrase is heard over and over again onboard a cruise ship: "Maybe I'll have just one more slice." Everything you have heard about the food on a cruise ship is true: It is wonderful. Don't even think about dieting while onboard the ship!

Have a healthy portion of baked Alaska. It is part of cruising tradition.

~~~~~

Since meals in the main dining room are included in the cost, a cruise ship is a good place to try different kinds of foods. Be adventurous—you might fall in love with an entirely new kind of cuisine.

~~~~~

Don't be hesitant to ask for something different if a dish is truly disappointing. The cruise staff want you to enjoy your meals.

~~~~~

Take your waiter's recommendations seriously. Waiters see a lot of food come and go and have an excellent idea of what the chefs do well and what they do not.

~~~~~

If your cruise ship offers specialty dining rooms, make your reservations on the first day of the cruise and ask for a table next to the window. These restaurants may have a surcharge, but they will be worth the money you pay.

Cruise ships will provide special meals for those on salt-free, sugar-free, low-fat, or diabetic diets. Your cruise agent can arrange this for you in advance—be sure to follow up the maitre d' once you are onboard.

By all means indulge in the midnight buffet, but take a small plate and sample a little of everything.

A good way to placate a bulging stomach is to take a stroll on the outside deck after each meal.

Very often, table mates in the dining room start the cruise as strangers and finish as good, lifelong friends. But if you sense a personality clash early on, don't hesitate—be pleasant during the meal, and later on discreetly arrange with the headwaiter or the maitre d' to be moved to another table.

If you have had a great time with your table mates, surprise everyone with a nice bottle of champagne on the last night of the cruise and toast to a future reunion.

Cruise ships often have "open sitting" lunches. These give you an opportunity to sit with passengers other than your usual dinner companions. It's another great way to meet fellow cruisers.

Try not to eat more than five meals a day!

Don't complain at your dinner table. It will bring everyone down.

When you arrive onboard, you will need to confirm your dining-room reservations. If the ship has two separate seatings and space is not available on the one you requested, contact the maitre d'. Sometimes a $10 tip will find you in the right time and place!

The barrage of cutlery at the dinner table may look overwhelming when you sit down to eat. Basically, the rule is to start with the outside silverware and work your way toward the plate as the courses progress. (Some ships offer a table-etiquette class for those who are really concerned about the proper use of silverware and table manners. This is not offered to insult anyone.)

Many of the larger ships offer pizzerias and other venues for casual dining. These places are more desirable when traveling with children or if you want a change from the formalities of the dining room. It is also a lot quicker.

Tables in the dining room are designed to accommodate two, four, six, eight, or ten people. If you are a large group or family, ask the maitre d' if you can be seated at adjoining tables.

Some cabins have a minibar. Just like in hotels, there is a charge for anything you eat or drink from it unless you are in a suite. All those traveling with you should be warned about this, as the cost can be substantial. Or you may find a tray left with bottled water and soft drinks. Generally, these are not complimentary—check before you open one.

Do not leave food lying around in your cabin. It is a continuous battle for the cruise lines to control insects onboard their ships.

If you or your children are used to eating dinner at 5:30 p.m. and the first seating for dinner is at 6:30 p.m., start adjusting mealtimes at home at least two weeks prior to the cruise.

If your cabin has a small refrigerator, you can use it to store fruit, yogurt, or other small snacks from the buffet for later in the day.

If your cruise line offers a choice of seatings, consider requesting the later seating. You can stay in port longer, sleep later in the morning, and participate in more of the late-evening activities—for many people, this lifestyle is a delightful change from their normal routines.

Many cruise ships offer alternative dining areas. If you do not wish to get dressed in formal attire, opt for the casual dinner buffet in the cafe upstairs.

~~~

Some cruise lines offer open-seating dining, which gives you the opportunity to dine anytime you wish and sit with whomever you would like. The only problem you might face is a long line of people wanting to eat at the same time. The busiest times are those following the captain's cocktail party or other public function.

Health and Beauty

Imagine sitting in a deck chair, soaking in the warm rays of the sun as a crew member walks around the pool area spritzing you with cool mist every fifteen minutes, or lounging in the Jacuzzi before receiving an hour-long massage. Those who have been on cruises have fond memories of the pampering they received onboard.

On some cruise ships, the health and beauty facilities are among the finest in the world. Some are more than 12,000 square feet in size! You can enjoy lifting weights, taking aerobics and yoga classes, receiving nutritional advice, and getting seaweed wraps over your entire body. The facilities offer all kinds of interesting treatments, so take advantage of their services.

Yoga, Pilates, and spinning classes are very popular and there's frequently a charge for attending.

~~~

Make your hair and beauty appointments early in the cruise. Even if the ship is large, the days at sea are extremely busy in this department. Massages are especially popular on cruise ships, so make an appointment early. With some cruise lines, these appointments can be made a couple of weeks prior to joining the ship. Ask your cruise agent.

Some of the massage therapists have a tendency to give a very light massage. If you prefer a deep-tissue massage, tell the attendant when you make your appointment and ask for the therapist who will accommodate your request.

Don't scream or shout around the pool area, and don't tolerate this behavior in your children. Many people take their afternoon siesta around the pool area.

If you are interested in keeping your daily workouts going, consult with the sports instructor onboard the ship to develop your own personal program to follow during the cruise.

When you get a haircut or other beauty treatment from one of the salon attendants, proper etiquette is to tip at the end of that service, as is standard practice on land.

The gym is usually very quiet when the ship is docked in port. If you don't like a lot of people around when you're working out, consider these times.

Most swimming pools are filled with filtered salt water. Use the shower facility next to the pool to rinse yourself. Also, if you used any snorkel equipment in the pool, rinse that off as well so the salt does not damage your mask or fins.

The Casino

Gambling is popular on most cruise ships, and the casinos can be very glamorous. As in every casino, there is always a chance to win—and lose. It can be exciting, especially if you are one of the lucky ones cashing in a bunch of chips or yelling "Bingo!" on the last day of the cruise. Good luck!

While some ports of call have casinos, the odds of winning in them are not any better than they are at sea.

Budget your gambling money carefully each day unless you want to find yourself washing dishes at the end of the cruise. Take only the amount of money you are willing to lose. The best odds for winning are not walking into the casino in the first place.

When gambling on the slots, try to grab the machines that are positioned at the end of a row, in view of everyone. They usually pay off more frequently than the rest of the machines.

Children under 18 years of age are not permitted to gamble in the casino.

The larger ships will have a MegaCash slot-machine area, lottery drawings, and heart-stopping bingo jackpots. Good luck!

Casino chips can be charged to your onboard credit account—but, of course, at the end the cruise, you do have to pay for them!

You may get a cash advance from the casino attendants simply by presenting your onboard charge card. This amount of money will be credited to your existing account.

Some ships are now so sophisticated that you can gamble right from your cabin using interactive television. Money is charged directly to your charge account, so set a limit on the amount you will spend.

Activities and Entertainment

You can never be bored on a cruise—unless you want to be. Some ships offer more than sixty activities each day! Some activities, such as art classes, are quiet and relatively solitary. Others, like organized games, are rowdy and sociable.

The great thing is, there's something for everyone. As one passenger commented, "I never thought I'd find a vacation where my husband could go and do his thing and I could do mine. It's the best vacation we've ever taken together!"

Pace yourself. Running from event to event will make you exhausted by the second day.

Take some time out to sleep in, lounge around, and kick off your shoes.

Regardless of what cabin category you have paid for, everyone has full access to the activities and events offered onboard the ship.

Carry a copy of the daily program so you know what time the activities are and where they are located.

Cruise lines schedule activities very tightly. When entering a theater or other area where a program may be in progress, do so quietly to avoid interrupting the enjoyment of others.

Many cruise ships offer vegetable-carving and ice-carving demonstrations. People who like to cook especially enjoy these, and kids find them fascinating as well.

Some cruise ships offer a religious service daily, while others provide them only on holidays. Your cruise agent can confirm with the cruise line whether a priest, minister, or rabbi will be onboard during your cruise.

Dance classes are usually offered during the cruise. Take advantage of them, even if you do not have a partner. There's something special about dancing onboard, and there's no charge (learning on land can cost a small fortune!).

Sea air makes many people especially hungry and sleepy. Take a power nap in the afternoon so that you have reserves of energy to enjoy all the wonderful things available in the evening.

The movie theater onboard the ship will be showing the latest feature films. Sometimes this room is particularly cool, so bring a sweater or shawl.

If foreign-language classes are offered, surprise your family at dinner with some of the new phrases you've learned.

Some ships hold a mock Kentucky Derby horse race. If you are traveling with your family or a group of friends, bid on a wooden horse. The winners receive a cash prize, and it is fun giving the horse a name and cheering it down the track.

Be pleasant when you are participating in any competitive activities on the ship. Having fun—not winning—is what it's all about. Besides, a prize like a plastic water bottle is not worth getting upset over!

There is nothing like an early morning jog on the top deck of the ship to start your day. You may even want to participate in the walk-a-mile program organized by the staff.

Most activities are free, but a few are not. Be sure to ask the staff in advance if you will have to pay to participate. Wine tasting and some craft activities may require a nominal fee.

Cruise lines often display elaborate artwork throughout their ships. Take time out to appreciate it. Some ships offer "tours" of the works and give a brief history of the artists.

Some cruise ships offer art auctions. If you collect art—and even if you don't—stop by to see what is available. Many times the prices of these pieces are a fraction of gallery prices. (If they serve complimentary champagne at these auctions, be careful how much you drink. You may end up buying something you later wish you hadn't.)

If you love the entertainment, reward the performers with a standing ovation. It's not easy to sing and dance on a moving ship!

If you would like to sit close to the stage during the evening shows, skip dessert to arrive earlier and nab the choice seats. You can always satisfy that sweet tooth at the midnight buffet.

Most engine rooms are off-limits to passengers, but you can sign up for the galley and bridge tours. Tours will give you a good look at the behind-the-scenes operations of a cruise ship. These are especially great activities for children.

The daily program may include "Friends of Dr. Bob and Bill W." This is the code for Alcoholics Anonymous meetings. AA members should contact the cruise director if these meetings are not listed in the daily program.

Onboard guest lecturers can give you valuable information about wildlife, geography, local culture, finances, bridge playing, life enrichment, color enhancement, and umpteen more topics. These lectures are complimentary, so take advantage of them.

If the sound is too loud in a particular lounge or theater, you may be sitting in front of a speaker or monitor. The central part of the room is usually best for sound and sight lines. If the volume is really too loud, contact the cruise director to sort out the problem.

When performers ask for volunteers to come up on the stage and participate in the show, do it. You may feel silly at first, but it will be the first thing you talk about when you get home.

Onboard Shopping

Many ships offer a veritable cornucopia of shopping opportunities. There are clothing boutiques, fine jewelry stores, perfume salons, shops with souvenirs and sundries, and everything in between. In fact, you could probably outfit yourself entirely onboard if you prefer to travel really light and bring along no luggage at all!

Most cruise lines provide duty-free specialty shops onboard their ships. (Duty-free means there are no taxes on the items.) Daily sales often sprout up, so stop in and see what is discounted each day.

Compare the prices of the merchandise sold onboard the ship with the same items sold in the ports of call. In most cases, you will find better prices onboard the ship.

Purchase some "logo wear" in the onboard shop. This is merchandise that has the name of the ship and cruise line on it. When you get home, all you have to do is wear it around and people will know you've been on a cruise.

If the toiletries you need are not provided in your cabin, they will probably be available in the gift shop.

Many cruise ships sell loose gemstones in one of their onboard shops. Often these offer exceptional quality and value, so take advantage of this if you plan to buy jewelry.

Photographers and Photographs

Photographs are an important part of your cruise experience. Bring along a good camera or video recorder – you'll be glad you did. Throw all caution to the wind and snap, snap, snap away.

There is no obligation to purchase any of the photographs taken by the photographers onboard the ship. Show them a smile whenever you see them.

Can't decide on which photos to buy? Ask the photo department to keep them "on file" for you and then select from all of them on the last day of the cruise.

If you are traveling with a group of friends or associates, make arrangements with the ship's photographer to meet everyone in a nice area of the ship. One that has a great background, such as a grand staircase or painting, is ideal. You may even consider having this picture taken in one of the ports of call. Don't forget to ask the photographer to give you a good price.

Buy a disposable or inexpensive digital camera for children over 5 years old traveling in your family, and let them take pictures throughout the cruise. When you return home, help them make a scrapbook.

Cruise-line photographers use digital cameras on most ships today. They can place any kind of background you would like to have on your pictures. Some ships are so advanced that the photos can be downloaded from the digital camera right into the television in your cabin. You can then choose which photographs you want to order from what you see on the screen.

Buy photographs of you and your special someone in the photo gallery. At the end of the cruise, have them placed in a nice album and give it to your partner as a special gift. It will be cherished for years.

The cruise line may provide a videographer to videotape passengers participating in various shore excursions and activities. Smile for the camera—you may just want to purchase a copy of the video before you leave the ship.

If you are traveling with your family, have a family portrait taken on one of the formal evenings. Ask the photographer to have copies made for each family member. That picture will be a wonderful reminder of your family adventure on the high seas.

Ask the photographer to take a photograph of everyone sitting at your dining table. Later, buy a copy for everyone and present it to them on the last night of the cruise.

Don't take your digital camera to the photo gallery and snap your photo just to avoid buying one. This is not only theft of copyright, it's tacky.

Purchase pictures taken by the ship's photographers that show the places and ports you have visited during your cruise. Some of these shots are better than the postcards you can buy from the local shops (and undoubtedly better than the average shutterbug's efforts).

Ports and Shore Excursions

ONE OF THE things that makes a cruise so unique, so different from any other vacation, is the opportunity to explore different ports of call and to go on a wide variety of shore excursions. There are, of course, tours of these ports, by foot, car, or bus; and shopping is always fun in a new place.

Some of your fondest memories of cruises are likely to be linked to special land excursions. Imagine going on a safari in Africa, riding in a helicopter over a volcano in Hawaii, floating in a dugout canoe down the Amazon River, walking on the Great Wall of China, holding a koala in Australia, walking among the penguins in Antarctica, or traversing a glacier in Alaska. Such exciting adventures are available to passengers at an additional cost, but they are wonderful memories that will last a lifetime.

Planning Ahead

Because your time is limited in each port of call, it is important to do some research and plan ahead.

Don't be afraid to ask your cruise agent a hundred questions, and check the Internet for additional information. What you learn can make a huge difference in the quality of your vacation.

Before leaving on the cruise, search through travel books and magazines to learn of any special festivals or holidays in your planned ports of call.

Each country's embassy and tourism offices can provide you with valuable information about the ports of call. You can get their phone numbers by calling the information operator in most major cities or checking their Web sites.

Be sure you've booked your shore excursions in advance through the cruise line's Web site. This helps ensure that you'll be able to participate, even if they are sold out when you arrive onboard the ship. Ask your cruise agent to give you your booking number, as you will need this to prebook these tours.

Some cruise lines offer a private club in the ports of call. These provide a great oasis when you are out shopping and need a relaxing place to sit and have a drink. Ask your shore-excursion staff if the cruise line has such a club.

The newer cruise ships are designed so that you can book your shore excursions right from your own cabin, using the remote control device (instructions are provided).

When was the last time you were on a picnic? Ask the executive chef or maitre d' if they could organize a picnic basket for you and your companions and then go relax and enjoy a simple picnic at a park in one of the ports of call. Expect a nominal charge for this service. (**Note:** This may not be available in all ports as some countries prohibit the importation of food from the ship.)

Sometimes a cruise ship is unable to dock in a particular port and the passengers are taken ashore in tender boats. The tendering operation is explained in the daily program, and most of the time the cruise director will make an announcement the night before. Be patient during the tender operations. Wait in one of the public lounges until you hear an announcement for your group to proceed to the gangway and go ashore. Passengers booked on a shore excursion are usually taken first.

It is very exciting to be outside when the ship is approaching or leaving any port of call. Walk around and take in the view.

Sometimes it is fun to stay onboard the ship when it is docked in port. The ship has an entirely different feeling when most of the passengers have left.

Be a good traveler: Learn a few key phrases—like "Please" and "Thank you"—in the language of each country you plan to visit.

If you are returning to a port of call that you have visited in the past, don't expect everything to be the same. Explore with an open mind.

Find out as many details about the shore excursions as you can. If the staff doesn't have the answers, ask them to find out for you. This will help prevent unpleasant surprises, such as going on an excursion that involves a half-mile hike up to a waterfall … when you twisted your ankle two days before.

Many island ports of call have beautiful resort hotels. Consider spending the day enjoying the facilities at one of these places. In most cases, the managers of these resorts welcome cruise-ship passengers, because they know they will be spending money on food, drinks, and souvenirs. They also hope that you'll return at a later date and stay at the hotel.

Some items sold in the more exotic ports of call are not allowed to be brought into your home country. Check with the shore-excursion staff or port lecturer to learn if any items in the port of call are included on this list.

Before going into port, check the time that you must be back onboard. (Usually it is thirty minutes before sailing time.) If you miss the ship, you will be responsible for getting yourself to the next port of call to rejoin the cruise—a very expensive mistake!

In some cases, cruise lines are not legally responsible for shore excursions; the tour operators they use for excursions may be independent contractors, thereby releasing the cruise lines of any liability. If you have an accident or mishap during an organized shore excursion, the cruise lines may help, but they are not legally obligated. Make sure that your insurance covers you for situations like this.

Ask the shore-excursion staff about the tipping policy in the ports you will be visiting. For example, in many places, tips for waiters are included in the restaurant check.

Be aware that people may badger you for handouts as you walk around some ports and tourist spots. If this would bother you excessively, you will probably be happier taking a guided bus or taxi tour of the port of call.

If you need to cancel a tour or shore excursion because of an illness, contact the tour office as soon as you can. In most cases, your money will be refunded, provided you have a legitimate excuse and a note from the ship's doctor.

At many ports you can book tours ashore that are similar to those you can book onboard. In many cases you can save money by doing this. However, the ship has no responsibility here. If something goes wrong, such as a bus breakdown, you will be on your own to get back to the ship on time, or to the next port, if you "miss the boat."

If the shore excursion is booked through the cruise line, and something goes wrong, the cruise line has the responsibility of getting you back to the ship. In most cases the ship will delay its departure if one of their shore excursions has been delayed getting back to the ship.

Any extra cost of booking your shore excursion through the cruise line is worth the peace of mind in knowing that if there is a problem, the cruise line will be made aware of the situation and be helping to resolve any difficulties.

Take your ship's daily program ashore with you. In most cases this has the time the ship will sail, the name and telephone number of the port agent, the number of the pier at which the ship is docked, and any other information that will help you remember the location of the ship. You don't want to find yourself on the other side of the island with no idea how to return to the ship.

Shopping!

The expression "Shop till you drop" is never so true as when you are on a cruise—the gift shops onboard the ship, the wide variety of retail shops in the ports of call, the vendors on the streets selling artifacts and souvenirs! Following these tips will help your shopping budget stretch further.

If the cruise line provides one, use the recommended shopping map. If anything should break or stop working when you get home, you'll have a guarantee from the cruise line that the store will replace it. (The cruise lines receive a commission from every purchase their passengers make.)

Some ports are terrible tourist traps. Ask crew members where the real bargain places are in town.

It is easy to get caught up in the excitement of an exotic port of call. To avoid throwing your money away, follow this rule: Don't purchase anything unless you first say to yourself, "If I were walking down the street back home and saw this in the window, would I buy it?" More times than not, the answer will be no.

Before you start to buy things in the first shop you see, look around and find out what the prices are in some of the other shops. You don't want to find out the bag you paid $70 for was only $50 at the store down the street.

In many parts of the world, bargaining is a form of shopping etiquette, especially in street markets and kiosks. In these situations, never accept the first price offered. Make a counteroffer of less than half what the vendors ask, and go from there to the price you are willing to pay.

~~~~~

Have fun while you are bargaining. This isn't life or death! The haggling should remain a friendly exchange. If the vendor (or you) gets too pushy or heated, it's time to leave.

~~~~~

While it's nice to get a good deal, be reasonable, and remember that people in many ports of call are extremely poor. Trying to chisel another dollar off the cost of a straw hat may mean that the vendor won't have dinner that night, while it's just pocket change to you.

~~~~~

Street vendors who follow you around pestering you to purchase their merchandise can best be handled with a firm "No." Avoid answering their questions and looking at them or what they are carrying.

~~~~~

When you walk into a shop, don't go directly to the item you want to buy or make a comment about how beautiful it is. This gives the merchant too much leverage in negotiating the price.

~~~~~

If you want to buy several items in one store, ask the manager to make a deal, such as 10 percent off everything.

~~~~~

In the more exotic ports, it is common for shop owners to give a very good deal on merchandise early in the morning. (They feel that the first sale is the most important of the day.)

When bargaining, once you decide on the price you want to pay, don't go higher. If the merchant does not accept your offer, begin to walk away. Often he will call you back and sell the merchandise at the price you quoted.

Avoid being ostentatious with your personal wealth. Do not wear expensive clothing and jewelry, and don't flash your cash around. Be discreet, not just to avoid being charged higher prices, but also to deter thieves.

Be aware: There is a tendency for shop owners to raise their prices when a cruise ship arrives in port. Always ask for a discount on the stated price.

Carry a small calculator to help you convert the exchange rate in foreign ports.

A small piece of inexpensive artwork from one of the local street vendors can serve as a special and unique memento of your trip.

In some places you can get great bargains toward the end of the tourist or cruising season.

When you buy something that will be shipped to your home, make sure that it is packed and the box is sealed and addressed before you leave the store. You don't want it to arrive a couple of weeks later and find that a different item has been sent, either on purpose or by mistake. Always pay with a credit card when you make purchases of this sort in case there is a dispute.

Take time to write the amount of your purchase in letters, not just numbers, to avoid any amount being changed. For example, on the bottom of the credit card receipt write "three hundred twenty dollars" if the amount is $320.

When making purchases in foreign countries using a credit card, ask the sales clerk what the rate of exchange is for that day and record it. Keep your sales receipt and compare it to your monthly credit card statement to ensure that you have not been charged more. If there is a discrepancy, call the credit card company to have them investigate the purchase. Avoiding this sort of problem is another reason for using the shops endorsed by the cruise line.

Sightseeing and Touring

Face it: You're going to act like a typical tourist when you go off on your sightseeing tours. A camera will be hanging around your neck, you'll be wearing Bermuda shorts or a muumuu and peering out from under a hat, and you'll be asking some of the same silly questions the group before asked. Even if you prefer to think of yourself as a sophisticated traveler and dress in the local garb, the people who live in the ports of call are going to take one look at you and think "tourist." Remember that everyone is a tourist outside their own country, so relax and enjoy the experience!

Treat yourself and your family to an unusual shore excursion—a helicopter ride, a submarine tour, or even a swim with the stingrays.

Everyone should snorkel at least once in their life. Give it a go!

Be polite to the people who live in the places you're visiting. While it's true that some may be trying to get you to buy something from them or to give them some money, other people may simply be curious about you, in the nicest possible way. Give them the benefit of the doubt.

Don't be an obnoxious foreigner. Remember that you are the guest and that the port of call is someone else's home—not your personal playground. Be respectful of the values and mores of the country.

Small children, and even most teenagers, are not particularly fond of cathedrals and museums unless it is a very quick tour. Remember this when planning your time ashore.

Use the restroom before leaving the ship. You never know when Mother Nature will call or how long it will be before you find a facility in port—or what shape it will be in!

~~~~~

If you have a bus driver and tour guide on your excursion, proper etiquette is to tip each person a couple of dollars when the tour is complete.

~~~~~

Don't wear beachwear in port—except on the beach. Would you wear a bikini or short-shorts while strolling down Main Street in your hometown?

~~~~~

Ancient ruins, wineries, and old cemeteries can get boring after a couple of hours, especially if the sun is extremely hot. Remember this when you are scheduling your excursions— don't try to pack too much in, especially in the afternoon.

~~~~~

Most city or island tours are two to three hours in length and consist of a bus ride, some shopping, and perhaps a snack. They are a great way to become familiar with the area.

~~~~~

When riding on a tour bus, try to sit in the front section so you can see more easily and have a smoother ride.

~~~~~

If for some reason you were not happy with your shore excursion, talk (politely!) with the shore-excursion manager. If your complaint is fair, you may be issued a partial refund or full credit.

Carry a small bottle of water with you in case you become thirsty. But don't drink too much, unless there is a restroom nearby.

Carry a snack such as a chocolate bar or nuts.

If you decide to hire a taxi for the entire day in port, you can save money if you have another couple or family ride with you. This will not only give you the opportunity to make friends with some fellow passengers, but it will also be a safer ride.

When visiting cathedrals and churches, respect the environment and keep your voice low.

Children love fish and animals. A visit to an aquarium, underwater sightseeing exhibit, wildlife park, or even a submarine ride will be a big hit.

The early morning hours offer more opportunities to see and photograph wildlife.

Collect a postcard from each port of call and make notes on the back, recalling your experience there.

Renting a Car

Many people prefer to rent a car and explore a new spot at their own pace. It's a chance to spend some quality time with the family or your beloved and absorb the flavor of a port of call. It's a wonderful feeling of independence and relaxation.

Get a map from the rental agency and ask for clear directions to the places you want to visit—and, more important, the way back to the agency. You don't want to spend all your time driving around in circles!

When booking a rental car, be sure to ask how far away the rental location is. In some ports, such as Lahaina, Maui, you must be taken by van to the other side of the island, a forty-minute to an hour ride, just to pick up your rental car. That's a loss of two hours of exploration time.

Know on which side of the road you will be driving. Most island countries drive on the left-hand side of the road, unlike North America.

Some countries may require you to pay a fee, as much as $25, for a nonresident driver's license (typically valid for several months). Remember this expense when deciding whether renting a car is a good way to get around.

Inspect every inch of your rental car before driving it away. If you see any dents or marks, make sure they are documented in your contract; otherwise, you might be charged a hefty sum when you return it.

Check with your credit card company before you rent a car—your rental insurance may be covered by the company, which will save you a lot of money. However, whenever there is more than one insurance company involved, especially from two different countries, you could be facing months of hassles and large amounts of paperwork. If you pay the Collision Damage Waiver, there will be only one insurance company from one country, and the hassle and paperwork is minimized.

Before you drive away, make sure you have the name and telephone number of the rental agent in the event you need to call for any reason.

Ask the agent if there are any areas in town that you should avoid because of construction or crime.

Ask the car-rental agent to point out on the map some residential areas that you can drive through. It's always interesting to check out the neighborhoods in a new port of call and see how people live.

Playing It Safe While in Port

Concerns for safety and security are not limited to the ship. You must always take precautions whenever you step off the ship and into another region of the world. Don't be paranoid, but do be careful and be watchful.

While swimming in the ocean or walking along the beach, wear water socks or other protective footwear. Sea urchins, rockfish, glass, and other "nasties" can be extremely painful—and sometimes deadly—if you accidentally step on them.

When walking around in port, especially in remote and exotic places, try to wash your hands frequently.

Drink only bottled water and other beverages, and avoid salads and other fresh vegetables.

Unless you can see how the ice cubes in your drink were prepared, assume that they were not made with boiled water, and don't have any.

In port, be cool—do not make political statements with your clothing. Don't wear T-shirts with religious symbols, flags, and so on.

If you go swimming, snorkeling, or scuba diving, look for posted signs that may caution you about a strong current or undertow. The excursion office onboard the ship can also advise you on safe areas to explore the underwater world.

When scuba diving or snorkeling, never place your hands in a dark hole. An eel may not be too happy having you invade its home!

If you get pricked by a sea urchin, pull the long spikes out of your skin and rub lemon or lime on the area. The acid from these fruits will help dissolve the spikes still embedded in your skin.

If you plan a shore excursion that involves a ride in a small airplane or helicopter, ask the shore-excursion staff about the safety record of the company. It is highly recommended that you book these types of excursions through the cruise line, not on your own.

Never leave valuables like a camera, watch, or iPod unattended while you are swimming in the ocean. Ask a friend or someone you can trust to watch it for you until you return. If no one's around to assist, seal it in a plastic bag and bury it in the sand under your towel or blanket.

Crowded marketplaces are a haven for pickpockets and thieves. Secure your purse, wallet, and jewelry.

Prepare the payment for your taxi driver while the cabby is driving, don't fumble with a bulging wallet while he looks on.

~~~~~~

When visiting areas where animals such as monkeys, birds, snakes, wild pigs, or kangaroos are not in cages, be cautious when petting or feeding them. Even if they appear to be cute and harmless, their bite or scratch could be dangerous.

~~~~~~

The ship may be docked overnight in a port. Do not walk around by yourself at night if there are not a lot of people around. Women and seniors especially should avoid walking alone in the evening.

~~~~~~

When venturing off the ship, attach an identification bracelet on your children with their name, blood type, any chronic illness, medications, allergies, mother's or father's name, telephone number at home, and the telephone number of the ship and the cruise line.

~~~~~~

Never carry a wallet in your rear trouser pocket. It is too easy for pickpockets to steal. Keep it in a front pocket of your pants or in an interior pocket of your jacket. A money belt is recommended.

~~~~~~

Carry your identification card from the ship.

~~~~~~

Instruct your children to contact a police officer or store clerk if they get lost in port.

Always lock your doors and close your windows when driving around in the ports of call—including in taxis.

Here's to Your Health and Well-Being

CRUISE LINES take the safety and security of their passengers and crew very seriously. Follow the specific guidelines provided to you onboard, and read these tips carefully. They literally can save a life—yours.

Safety and Security

They say that rules are meant to be broken, but this is one adage that definitely does not apply at sea. The safety of all people onboard a ship is paramount, and passengers are expected to abide by the rules and regulations established by the particular cruise line as well as by maritime law. It cannot be stressed enough: Safety first!

Security is of the utmost importance on cruise ships. Be patient if you have to go through the same rigorous screening at the pier that you might have experienced at the airport just an hour or two before. Everyone agrees it's better to be safe.

~~~~~~

Let's make one thing perfectly clear: You *do not* have to worry about the ship capsizing in a storm! They may be tossed around a bit, but cruise ships are built to survive the most severe weather.

~~~~~~

The captain will not risk the lives of any passengers or crew members. Should threatening weather or political conditions crop up in a particular port or region, the itinerary of the cruise may be changed. If this happens, go with the flow. Don't grumble—such shifts in plans are made for your safety.

~~~~~~

Look around the cabin for any objects that might pose a danger to your little tykes, such as electrical outlets, sharp furniture edges, or things that can be pulled down and might hit them on the head. This is usually not a problem on newer ships, but if any hazards are found, contact the cabin steward.

Check the life jackets in your cabin. Are they properly maintained, with a whistle, proper ties, and a light (when the jacket hits salt water, the emergency light attached to the jacket automatically goes on)? Sometimes these items are missing. If this is the case, ask your cabin steward to solve the problem.

Should you detect a fire or smell smoke, don't hesitate: Immediately call a crew member or press the nearest fire-alarm switch.

It is unlikely that a person will fall overboard, but if this should happen, throw the nearest life ring into the water and contact a crew member at once.

After participating in the lifeboat drill on the first day of the cruise, look down the hallway near your cabin and locate the closest fire extinguisher and emergency call buttons.

Cabin doors are equipped with special guards or wedges to keep them from swinging open or slamming shut. Use them! You never know when the ship will suddenly list.

Never clean your pipe by banging it on the side of the ship. Burning tobacco could blow back onboard and cause a fire. For the same reason, don't throw lit cigarettes or cigars overboard. Put them out in the receptacles provided.

It's best to wear medium-height or lower heels onboard rather than high heels. A sudden movement of the ship could cause you to turn your ankle and become injured.

Use the closets, not the fire sprinklers suspended from the ceiling, to hang your clothing. Garments dangling from the sprinklers could block water from extinguishing a fire in your cabin—obviously, a life-threatening situation for everyone onboard.

Remember an "old salts" rule—one hand for the ship, one for you. Always use the ship's handrails when walking outside on the deck, as a sudden motion of the ship could cause you to lose your balance.

Many doorways and thresholds on the ship have elevated ledges to cross over. Be extra careful when walking through them.

Make sure that your children know what to do if the emergency signal sounds. The instructions are posted on the back of cabin doors and all around the ship.

Designate a spot to meet in case of emergency.

In the health club, take special care when using free weights over your head. A sudden movement of the ship could cause you to lose your balance and drop the weights.

Never, never make jokes onboard about a bomb scare or a fire. Unfortunately, anyone can be a suspect for terrorism. As in an airport, such "jokes" will be taken seriously, and the crew is likely to hustle you to a security office for questioning. At the very least, this will be unpleasant and embarrassing. You may also be subject to a fine and criminal prosecution. Your children should also understand the serious ramifications of making these kinds of statements.

Avoid using the swimming pool if the seas are rough. The force of the waves could push you into the side of the pool and cause a very serious injury.

Do not light candles or incense while onboard. This is strictly forbidden by maritime regulations. (If there is candlelight in the dining room, it's never an open flame.)

Should there be an emergency, you will be told where to go. Do not push or shove other passengers, and follow the instructions given by the crew members in charge of the muster station (the place where you gather).

~~~~~~

Do not take the elevator during an emergency situation. If for some reason it is hard for you to navigate stairs, contact the information desk and register your name and cabin number on a special emergency-assistance sheet. If something should happen, the crew will come to your cabin and help you to a safe location.

~~~~~~

Always use caution when walking on the gangway. Do not feel pressured to walk fast just because other people are waiting behind you. Make sure each step you take is stable, and use the handrails for assistance.

~~~~~~

Ask the cabin steward what the wattage is in your cabin or bathroom before plugging in electric razors, toothbrushes, or hair dryers. You don't want to get hurt or cause a fire. If you need a converter, the steward will provide one. Nearly all the newer ships have 110-volt outlets.

~~~~~~

It is common for black soot to blow out of the ship's smoke-stack. Be sure you've checked the deck chairs and lounges before you sit down on them.

~~~~~~

Passengers are not allowed to bring visitors onboard. Don't give the security staff on the gangway a hard time when they refuse to let your friends on the ship or check your identification. They are only doing their job, and it's to protect you.

Do not bring illegal drugs onto the ship. If you are caught, you will be released to the local authorities and face criminal charges. Surely experiencing prison life in one of the ports of call is not the sort of sightseeing you have in mind!

In the event that you are harassed by a passenger or crew member, contact the hotel manager and ask for help. Cruise lines will not tolerate such behavior, and the ship's security officers will enforce this policy.

Tell children to contact the nearest crew member should they get lost onboard the ship. An announcement can be made so you can meet them at the information desk.

Lock the door each time you leave your cabin. (If you happen to lock yourself out, the purser's desk will arrange to have someone come by and open the door, or you can ask the nearest cabin steward for a hand.)

Never accept packages from strangers to bring onto the ship, even if they say that someone onboard is expecting it.

If there is a safe in your cabin, use it to secure your valuables, including your travel documents. If your cabin does not have a safe, ask at the purser's desk to use a safe-deposit box. These boxes are usually available at no extra cost.

Medical Care

A cruise ship is one place where you don't have to worry about receiving medical attention. Nearly every cruise ship afloat has a full hospital facility, including a pharmacy and X-ray machines, and a professional staff trained to take care of most medical emergencies.

If you expect to need attention from the onboard doctor, be sure you have your medical documents with you. Your cruise agent should also inform the cruise line beforehand that you will be requiring medical assistance while you are onboard.

~~~~~~~

Tape your name and cabin number on the stems of your eye-glasses and on the inside of their case—thus, in the event you leave them somewhere, lost-and-found will be able to reunite them with you quickly. As an extra precaution, bring a spare pair of glasses or contacts and, if possible, your prescriptions.

~~~~~~~

People who use oxygen should book direct flights whenever possible, and they should alert the onboard medical personnel as soon as they embark.

~~~~~~~

If you use the doctor's services or the hospital facility onboard the ship, you will be charged. Your medical insurance should cover this—but be sure to check with your insurance company before leaving on the cruise. Get everything in writing!

Most doctors recommend that pregnant women do not go on a cruise in their third trimester.

Keep your medicine clearly labeled, and bring along copies of your prescriptions. If you fly through several time zones on your way to joining the ship and you need to take medication at timed intervals, consult your physician or pharmacist to help you plan an easy-to-follow schedule.

Vaccinations may be required if you are traveling to exotic ports of call. Find out from your cruise agent, as you will be required to show proof of your vaccination before embarking.

You can obtain a recent sanitation report of the ship you will be cruising on by contacting the Centers for Disease Control and Prevention. Inspections are made at least once a year, and for a ship to be in good standing, it must score eighty-six points or more, out of a possible one hundred.

Being on a cruise ship can motivate you to work out in the health facility, dance the night away in the disco, or participate in an invigorating shore excursion. If you are unaccustomed to regular exercise, take it easy at first!

Preventing Seasickness

Seasickness can really put a damper on your cruise. Ask your doctor before you leave what anti-seasickness medicines will be most appropriate for you. Over-the-counter medications often are a good thing to pack if you can't get to the doctor. Even old seadogs occasionally get seasick. Some tried and sometimes true remedies include ginger ale and dry crackers, green apples, massage, and acupressure bands worn around your wrist. And don't forget that some fresh air is always helpful. Snuggle into a deck chair and try to relax.

You will help prevent motion sickness if you book a cabin in the center part of the ship—center both horizontally and vertically. (The forward end of the ship, as well as the cabins on the top decks, have more pronounced movement.)

If you become seasick and your children don't, ask one of the youth counselors onboard to help keep them entertained for the day. They are usually pretty good about that.

Most cruise ships are designed with stabilizers, located toward the front of the ship, that extend on both sides just below the waterline. In the event of a storm or rough seas, the stabilizers—as their name implies—help to keep the ship steady.

Pediatricians should be consulted before the cruise to provide motion-sickness tablets for the kids.

When the seas are rough, don't read a book, write postcards, or do anything else that focuses your attention downward. This may cause you to get seasick.

Don't eat or drink too much. That nausea you're feeling could be indigestion or a hangover. Remember, all things in moderation. It doesn't mean no dessert, just not the entire cake.

Preventing Sunburn

Too many cruisers have spent their long awaited vacations lying in bed in helpless torment—burned to a crisp in their zeal to get a tan. Take precautions! There are ways to get a nice glow without doing yourself in.

The sun is very deceiving on a ship. Because the breezes are blowing, keeping you cool, passengers tend to think they are not getting blasted by ultraviolet rays. Always use plenty of sunscreen or sunblock.

In the first couple of days, use a sunblock with a SPF of twenty-five or higher, and do not lie in the sun longer than an hour.

Always, always wear a hat!

Passengers have been known to get serious burns on days when the sky is cloudy. Don't let the overcast sky fool you—wear protection.

Apply sunscreen or sunblock after each dip in the pool or ocean. (Consider getting a spray for quicker application.)

Don't forget to apply sunblock on your lips, ears, and feet!

The beach and poolside are not the only places you have to be concerned about getting a sunburn. Put on plenty of sunblock when on a shore excursion, shopping, or strolling onboard.

If you plan to wear strapless or backless evening wear, apply sunscreen or sunblock during the day over the appropriate areas so you won't have unattractive tan lines or burns.

When cruising through the Panama Canal or other regions where the sun's rays are extremely intense, use an umbrella in addition to sunscreen or sunblock. Temperatures there can reach well over 120 degrees F (49 degrees C)!

If you go snorkeling or scuba diving, put extra sunblock on your neck, back, arms, and legs. The sun's rays can go directly through the water, so wear a T-shirt to protect your back.

If you plan on doing a lot of snorkeling, consider investing in a Lycra body suit, available at most Scuba shops.

Use aloe-vera gel or cream to relieve sunburn pain. Products with aloe vera are also good moisturizers.

Cruises for Families
and Other Special Groups

WHERE CAN THE Red Hat Ladies, couples seeking romance, specialists in Byzantine archaeology, and your globetrotting grandparents from London all find the ideal vacation? On a cruise, of course! (Did you really think I'd say something else?) Virtually all kinds of groups can find a cruise that will meet the interests and needs of their members.

Families

"Family vacation." Sounds like an oxymoron, doesn't it? (Think "honest politician," "military intelligence.") Those who've been there can attest that a holiday with the kids can be more trick than treat.

But families are by far the biggest special-interest group in the cruising industry, and no wonder: It's a wonderful way to travel as a family! Not only is it exciting and exotic, but a cruise can be amazingly inexpensive. Many cruise lines offer family discounts and packages. And the all-inclusive nature of most cruises has a valuable psychological benefit: It relieves that nagging irritation you feel when you are constantly digging into your wallet to pay for a meal—for five.

Perhaps even more appealing than the financial benefits is that cruising can be so worry-free for parents. There's a lot of space, but the kids can go only the length and breadth of the ship—a relatively secure environment. In addition, many ships offer a cornucopia of facilities and activities that will provide something of interest for everyone. Thus, as the parents sip Campari on their private veranda, serenely watching island peaks go by, their 14-year-old is having a blast playing water volleyball, while their 10-year-old goes wild in the video arcade or learns the rudiments of watercoloring.

There are many Web sites specializing in family cruises. Have a look at www.cruisesforfamilies.com or www.family cruises.com.

When you are planning the cruise, include every family member in the discussion. Make a wish list of everyone's choices and communicate the information to your cruise agent.

Family cruises need not be limited to the immediate family, of course. A cruise ship is a great venue for a family reunion. It's also a wonderful way to spend quality time with grandparents, cousins, close family friends, and so on.

Babysitting can be arranged at the information desk. Reserve a sitter as soon as you can. Some cruise lines charge for evening babysitting.

If there are ten or more people traveling from the same city and you need air transportation to get to the ship, have your cruise agent arrange a group rate with one of the airlines. This could be many dollars less per person than the cruise line's airfare.

If possible, pack each child's belongings in a separate piece of luggage.

When packing, remember to bring a favorite stuffed animal, toy, or storybook for each child. This "security blanket" will help the child adjust to the ship.

Put together a "goodie bag" for your children that contains projects to occupy them on the plane, while waiting to embark or disembark the ship, and whenever else they may get restless.

Bring along a map of the world. Each night, show your children the places you expect to be passing by or visiting the next day. Enrich their understanding of where they're traveling with facts about each place and with historical and cultural information from a travel guidebook.

If your child is not toilet-trained or if you have children under the age of 3, they cannot participate in the youth program provided by the cruise line. However, babysitting services are available.

Cruise ships are very different from most people's surroundings in normal life. To help your children feel comfortable, walk around the ship with them after unpacking and get familiar with the facilities.

Even 8-year-olds enjoy the thrill of spending recklessly. Give your children some money to blow on their vacation.

Ask one of the kids to be responsible for assembling a family scrapbook of the cruise, with photos, ticket stubs, excursion brochures, and so on.

To lend structure to the cruise, assign each child a chore. An older sibling might babysit the twins late at night while the parents dance in the disco. For their part, the twins can put away all the kids' toys and clothes each evening before bed.

Have some brightly colored T-shirts with the name of the ship or some special symbol (for security reasons, no kids' names, please) made up for each family member. Not only will this serve as a nice memento, but it will help you find each other at a glance, onboard and off.

Most cruise lines that focus on family cruising will have cribs available. If you need one for your baby, ask your cruise agent to request one for you.

If the family is in two or more cabins, buy a pair of walkie-talkies so you can communicate back and forth, both on the ship and in a busy shopping port. The kids are going to love it and they help you keep track of everyone.

Most ships offer a parent/child orientation with the youth supervisors on the first day of the cruise. The staff will provide detailed information about the programs and help the kids choose those that are right for them.

Give the children some basic rules of etiquette to follow when they are onboard the ship. (The last thing you want is the management calling to complain about your child's behavior.) Emphasize the importance of the safety instructions. Also remind them that the ship's elevators are not playthings.

The drinking age onboard most cruise ships is 18, because the ships will be sailing in international waters. Teenagers should know that they will be asked for ID if they order alcohol.

Keep a notepad in the cabin so everyone can record where they can be found throughout the day.

Some cruise lines let children travel free if they stay in their parents' cabin. This will not be very appealing for some couples (or for their kids, for that matter), but for those who expect to use the cabin as a mere pit stop, it's a great deal!

When the ship is in port, older teenagers who want to venture off by themselves should be given a designated time and place to meet with their parents. All family members should know the name of the ship in case they get lost.

The cruise program for the following day arrives in your cabin the preceding evening. At bedtime, plan the next day's schedule with the children. Find at least one activity that the entire family can participate in together. Also insist that everyone meet for dinner. It may be the only time you are all together during the cruise.

If your cabins are next to wild party-givers or particularly loud lovers, you might want to ask the hotel manager if it is possible to be moved. Along the same lines, expect courtesy from the kids—don't let them disturb their neighbors.

They shouldn't be allowed to shriek, run in and out slamming doors, jump on the beds, pound on walls, and so on.

Hand-draw a simple map of the ship for younger children so it is easier for them to find their cabin. Also, let them tape a little drawing to the outside of their cabin door so they can see their cabin from way down the hall.

Singles

In recent years, cruise lines have put together many packages meant to appeal particularly to single people. Singles are a unique breed of cruisers. They are often exceptionally adventurous, joining in many activities with zeal and good humor. Sometimes people without partners opt for a cruise geared toward singles because they often feel excluded in our couples-oriented society; on the cruise— or at least in various programs and activities— they can be among the majority for a change.

Sometimes single passengers can cruise at a lower rate during the off-seasons. Ask your cruise agent to look into these fares.

Beware of ship's crew who make marriage proposals or make you feel like you are the love of their life. Chances are they used the same line on another passenger on the cruise before—if not the night before! Enjoy their attentions by all means, but be realistic.

If you are accustomed to a queen- or king-size bed at home, ask the cabin steward to push the twin beds together.

If you are an older single man, you might qualify to cruise for free or at a considerable discount as a gentleman host. You can find out more about this program by calling the cruise lines directly.

If you don't want to be bothered by other passengers looking for a date, wear a wedding ring. This should keep most (but probably not all!) potential love interests away.

Opt for elegance rather than exhibitionism in your clothing. Extremely provocative swimwear and evening wear will likely attract more pests than princes.

If you are interested in meeting other single passengers, ask the maitre d' to seat you at a dining table with single guests.

Gays and Lesbians

The gay and lesbian cruise travel market has tripled in the past decade. Many cruise lines make a special effort to design packages that will appeal to people with nontraditional lifestyles.

There are many companies that offer gay and lesbian cruises. Before you book your cruise, you may want to check out www.aquafest.com or www.rainbowcruises.com.

Buy a gay/lesbian guidebook to the destinations to which you will be traveling, before leaving on your cruise.

Ask the shore-excursion staff if they can recommend different places in port that you can explore. Many times they will know of gay establishments.

Be patient, not angry or rude, to passengers who frown upon your homosexuality or bother you in any way.

When you arrive onboard the ship, ask the cruise director to help you set up a gathering. Ask her to print in the daily program: "Friends of Dorothy's Get-Together" or "Pink-Triangle Party." Most homosexuals will understand this code and come to the festivities to meet other gay people early in the cruise.

Seniors

Many older people today have not only the time but the financial resources to cruise the world in style—and many are doing so. Two-week, two-month, even six-month cruises to exotic ports of call around the world beckon to these discerning travelers.

Generally speaking, the longer the cruise, the older the passengers onboard the ship.

Some cruise lines sail more seniors than others. Study cruise-brochure photos carefully—what age are the passengers in those smiling photos?

If you are looking for a relaxing cruise with no children running around the ship, ask your cruise agent to suggest a couple of options.

When cruising during the holidays or summer, you can expect several hundred children (or more!) to be onboard many of the larger cruise ships.

If you are used to going to bed or eating dinner early, start adjusting your clock to the ship's schedule a month before you go on your cruise.

Don't be afraid to talk to passengers of all ages. One of the advantages of a cruise is the opportunity to meet all sorts of people, of all ages—and for them to have the pleasure of getting to know you.

Beware of pushy taxi drivers in some ports of call. They may promise a certain fare and then try to take advantage of you because you're a senior citizen. Try to establish a fare in advance (in some countries, the government sets the rates). If the cabby goes over that fare, get one of the port agents to sort out the conflict.

Honeymooners and Other Romantics

A kiss on the cheek while strolling on the deck and an intense gaze across the dining-room table are just a couple of the subtle ways honeymooners and romantics express their affection when sailing onboard a love boat. Cruising is the ideal vacation for those who want to enhance or rekindle their relationships.

There are many terrific Web sites that offer honeymoon cruises at a discount. A couple of examples are www.liberty travelhoneymoons.com and www.honeymoonvoyages.com.

A great way to begin your cruise, and a nice way to say "I love you" to the person you will be cruising with, is to order a bon voyage gift and have it waiting in the cabin when you arrive on the ship. Ask your cruise agent to arrange the gift.

Everyone loves a lover—within reason. Spare your fellow passengers the details of your sex life. They really are not interested in watching you make out in the pool or writhe against each other on the dance floor.

If you want to impress your special someone, ask your cruise agent or the shore-excursion staff to inquire about limousine service in one of the ports of call. It's a great feeling to walk down a gangway in a glamorous island port and know that the shiny limousine is all yours, waiting to escort you and your loved one around the island in utter comfort. Go all the way—arrange to have strawberries and champagne waiting inside!

If you are fairly recently married or have different last names, bring along a copy of your marriage certificate for Immigration. You may need it as a form of identification.

Where better to get married than on a glorious cruise ship? Ask your cruise agent to inquire with the cruise line about this option for tying the knot.

Sometimes you can get married on land and have the reception onboard while the ship is docked in port. Your guests will be thrilled, and once they leave, you and your sweetheart can begin your honeymoon. Your cruise agent can help with the arrangements.

If you wear your wedding dress to the ship, ask the cruise director if it can be stored in one of the costume areas. Usually there is room, and it can hang there, protected and secure, until you disembark.

Your cruise agent can help you arrange to renew your wedding vows onboard the ship. (If you feel impassioned once onboard, the cruise director may also be able to assist you!)

Many cruise ships now have an onboard wedding chapel. If you would like to get married onboard a ship, your cruise agent can arrange the ceremony through the cruise line's special wedding department. There is usually a charge for the renewal of vows or wedding service. Prices vary with how many amenities you decide to include.

Ask your cabin steward to place a red rose on your partner's pillow when preparing your cabin for the evening. Include a note written by you suggesting a bit of fun and frolic. (Don't forget to give your cabin steward a couple of dollars for helping out.)

Sit in the Jacuzzi late at night with a bottle of champagne, a bowl of strawberries, and some soft music. Ask your cabin steward to help arrange the setup. (A nice tip would be appropriate here).

If you know your loved one's favorite song, talk to the musicians beforehand and have them play the song while you enjoy a cocktail or dance in one of the lounges.

Take a walk outside late at night and steal a kiss in the moonlight. If the fireworks start exploding, go to your cabin—do not attempt to climb into one of the lifeboats!

If your cabin has a veranda or balcony, request dinner to be brought to your stateroom, and dine outside with your special someone. It is very romantic!

Buy each other something special in the onboard gift or jewelry shop to remember your wonderful time together.

People with Special Needs

Most cruise ships are wheelchair-friendly, and so are the crew and staff who work on them. Don't hesitate for one minute if you are physically or otherwise challenged and worried about whether you will be alright on a cruise. Go for it, and have the time of your life!

Not all cruise ships are built to accommodate physically challenged passengers. The newer vessels, though, have terrific cabins, and it is easy to access all areas of the ship. Make sure your cruise agent has specifically asked the cruise line about this, and get confirmation in writing.

Most cruise lines require physically challenged passengers to sail with an able-bodied companion. Be sure that the person you are traveling with understands the responsibilities before getting onboard the ship.

If you don't have a traveling companion, call your local hospital and ask if there are any retired nurses or aides who might be interested in going with you. You will have no problem finding one—especially, of course, if you are paying for the cruise.

Some cruise lines allow Seeing Eye dogs onboard their ships, but you must get written permission in advance. Your cruise agent can arrange this.

A limited number of wheelchair-accessible cabins are available on cruise ships. Try to make your cruise travel arrangements at least a year in advance.

If you are hearing-impaired, make sure your cruise companion lets you know about any important onboard announcements.

The Society for the Advancement of Travel for the Handicapped (SATH) offers advice to people with disabilities who wish to travel. Call (212) 447-7284 for a free copy of SATH's newsletter.

Inform the hotel staff of your disability. In the event of an emergency, a special rescue party will go to your cabin and assist in taking you to your emergency boat station.

If you are physically challenged, contact the cruise director. The cruise staff will then be informed, and you can feel more comfortable about participating in entertainment and activities.

It is very difficult for passengers in wheelchairs to go ashore when the ship is tendering. The staff at the information desk can help arrange preboarding for you or set up a better time for you to use the tender boats.

On bus tours in ports of call, often a tour guide explains the sights over a microphone system. Remember this when booking excursions if you are hearing-impaired.

Business Meetings, Clubs, and Larger Groups

Business meetings and conferences onboard cruise ships are increasing in popularity. Where else can you watch the head speaker stand at a podium and sway from side to side? Cruise ships are equipped with the latest technologies that allow nearly any kind of group, business committee, or club to gather together and conduct business. Next time your organization wants to hold a big-destination meeting, suggest a cruise ship!

Large groups can receive a substantial discount on a cruise. Have your cruise agent contact the group department at the cruise line you wish to sail with. Have your cruise agent arrange with the cruise line to set up a desk in the lobby area on the ship. This will give everyone traveling in your group a focal point and central area in which to meet.

Ask your cruise agent to book a section of cabins in the same general area of the ship. This will give you an opportunity to keep some cabin doors open and visit from cabin to cabin.

(Remember to respect the privacy and quiet times of those not involved in your party.)

Your cruise agent and the group department of the cruise line will be able to advise you on specific arrangements for conferences, seminars, dinners, and so on. It is no more complicated than arranging a group meeting or conference on land—but it is so much more memorable and satisfying an event!

Family reunions, corporate business meetings, high school reunions, and all kinds of large groups are choosing a cruise as their venue for meeting. Contact the cruise lines directly for information on how you can design a cruise that best suits the needs of a large group.

Fund-raising is important to many nonprofit organizations, churches, schools, and families in a financial crisis. If your organization is interested in a cruise fund-raiser, contact your favorite cruise agent.

Have identifying tags, T-shirts, or other mementos made in advance and pass them out to the group members as they arrive onboard.

Contact the ship's photographer to organize a group photograph.

When the Party's Over

YOU'VE EATEN YOUR last supper, packed your souvenirs in the dirty laundry, and sat on your suitcase to get it shut. Ready or not, it's time to go home.

Don't be too sad—as my grandma used to say, "If you don't leave, how can you come back again?" That said, it is true that you will probably feel a little blue. But you may have happier memories of the cruise as a whole if you take a few simple steps to make the transfer home more relaxed and your readjustment to real life less jarring.

Packing Up

It will be a lot easier to pack up at the end of the cruise than it was to pack for the cruise. Since you will probably be cleaning all your clothes when you get home, wrinkling and organization won't be such an issue. Go ahead—throw everything in pronto so that you can enjoy every last minute of your adventure!

Don't forget to gather all your personal items from your cabin safe or from the safe-deposit box at the purser's desk. If you forget something on the ship, contact the cruise line's corporate office. (Unfortunately, not all items are turned into the lost-and-found, so remember to check everywhere before you leave.)

You will be asked to place your luggage outside your cabin door the night before disembarkation; the ship's staff will take it to a central area for distribution. Make sure you have kept a change of clothing for the following day—you don't want to walk down the gangway wrapped in a shower curtain!

Roll up each piece of dirty laundry as tightly as possible and place it around any breakable items (you might prefer to carry some of these items with you).

Pack all valuables in your carry-on bags.

Disembarkation

Getting the passengers and luggage off the ship is typically a long and tiring process because the ship has to get clearance from the port authorities and you may have to go through Immigration and Customs. Instead of getting frustrated, use the time to take a last stroll around the ship, enjoy a good-bye conversation with your new friends, and admire the views of the port where the ship has docked.

A day or so before you leave the ship, the cruise director will hold a briefing explaining all the procedures to follow regarding disembarkation. At least one person from each family should attend this talk, as the information will provide a smooth transition for you to leave the ship. This briefing will also give you an opportunity to ask questions. Bring a paper and pen and note the most important points.

You can realistically count on two to three hours of waiting around before the actual disembarkation from the ship begins. Keep a crossword puzzle, cards, or a book handy to amuse yourself during this time.

Physically challenged passengers and any other guests needing assistance are given priority disembarkation privileges. Please don't abuse this privilege if you don't really qualify for it.

If you are on the air-sea package, you will be transferred to the airport by the cruise-line representatives. The earlier your flight, the sooner you will disembark from the ship and be transferred.

On the morning of disembarkation, breakfast hours will be moved back one hour. This will be your last opportunity to eat before leaving the ship, so if you want breakfast, plan on getting up early.

Passengers are not allowed to disembark from the ship until all the luggage has been taken off the vessel and arranged in the terminal building, usually according to a number or colored tag that you placed on your bags the night before. This procedure can take a good couple of hours. Be patient! Getting irritated won't speed it along.

Porters will be available in the luggage terminal to help you transfer your bags. It is customary to tip these gentlemen $1 per bag.

Sometimes passengers leave a ship and their cruise with a bad impression because the disembarkation process was too long or poorly organized. You can help the cruise line and yourself if you eat a leisurely breakfast, relax in your cabin or one of the public lounges, and plan an activity to amuse yourself until it is time to leave.

Don't gather around the gangway area and talk to the staff in charge of helping with disembarkation. Say your good-byes early so that they can get their jobs done and speed the process up for everyone.

Room service and bar service are discontinued on the morning of disembarkation.

When the captain receives clearance from the port authorities, disembarkation can begin. In some cases, not only will you have to wait for this clearance, but you will also have to pass through Customs.

If there is a "lucky comment-card drawing" at the end of your cruise, make sure you enter. Sometimes cruise lines give away a discount on a future cruise. Also, be as honest as you can with your comments—the cruise lines will appreciate any advice you can give to better their product.

After Your Cruise

When your cruise is finished, you arrive home and begin your reentry into real life. Slowly, you will begin to get into your daily routine again—whether you want to or not. But something will feel different. You may find that you are craving something unlike anything you've ever hungered for before. It isn't a sick feeling, but an overpowering sense of want, desire, and obsession. It is a condition called *cruise-itis*. (The technical name is "frequent floaters disease.") The symptoms? You can't stop talking about your cruise. You thrive on other people's cruise stories, and you even look for ways to top them. You go to your cruise agent, start looking at cruise brochures again, and begin planning your next cruise.

This phase is very common, and the symptoms last only a couple of weeks. Many people go through it, so don't panic. Eventually, you will get back to normal and will even enjoy your "real" life again. You gradually become your old self—that is, until the next cruise.

If you are on a post-land package, you may begin your tour immediately after you disembark from the ship. This means you may not see your hotel until that evening. Make sure you have had a good breakfast, are wearing comfortable clothing and shoes, and have had a stop at the restroom before the tour.

Some cruise agents do a tremendous amount of work to see that you have the best cruise possible. If you thoroughly enjoyed your cruise, why not send a thank-you note or perhaps give your agent a souvenir from one of the ports of call? These gestures are really appreciated.

Call the cruise agency or e-mail them with feedback about your cruise, good and bad. This helps them to know whether or not to recommend that cruise ship or cruise line again.

Join the cruise line's repeat-passenger club. On your next cruise with that cruise line, you may receive some nice gifts, an invitation to a special cocktail party, or early check-in at the pier.

If you were happy with the service you received from one particular staff member, write a letter to the cruise-line corporate office and commend the cruise line for hiring such a professional person. These letters carry a tremendous amount of weight, especially when there is a possibility of promotion of a crew member.

If your cruise was a complete disaster, explain the details to your cruise agent. She will contact the cruise line and attempt to get some kind of discount or refund if the situation merits. If you feel your cruise agent was the reason for the disaster, use the tips in the section on planning your cruise to find a different cruise agent for next time.

Ask your cruise agent to let you know about discounts on future cruises.

If you are interested in becoming a cruise agent yourself and would like to take a cruise course online, go to www.cruise training.net or www.keisercareer.edu. It can be a wonderful way to supplement your income and also receive substantial discounts on future cruises.

Finding Employment on Cruise Ships

While it is wonderful to work on a cruise ship, it is not suited for everyone. Cruise lines hire professionals, not just individuals who want to get away from their boring jobs at home and work for a couple of weeks or months. Working onboard a ship is completely different from vacationing on one. It takes high energy, strong commitment, and long hours. And remember, you won't be traveling in a cabin with a veranda, eating in the passenger dining rooms, or playing bingo.

Some cruise lines receive 200 to 300 photos and résumés each month from people seeking employment. Because the demand is so great, the employees who work on cruise ships must be extremely service-oriented and have brilliant customer-service skills. They must also have some kind of training or experience in the department in which they hope to work.

Beware of scam operators promising jobs on cruise ships. No one can promise you a job except the cruise line itself. Before you order any type of book regarding employment opportunities on cruise ships, ask for the copyright date, the name and reputation of the author, and detailed information about its contents. Sometimes, even if the book has 300 pages, only 20 of those pages are related to cruise ships, and even those pages could be outdated or irrelevant.

Cruise Line Directory

American Canadian Caribbean Line
www.accl-smallships.com
(800) 556-7450

American Cruise Lines
www.americancruiselines.com
(800) 814-6880

Azamara Cruises
www.azamaracruises.com
(877) 999-9553

Carnival Cruise Lines
www.carnival.com
(888) 227-6482

Celebrity Cruises
www.celebrity.com
(800) 647-2251

Costa Cruise Lines
www.costacruises.com
(877) 882-6782

Cruise West
www.cruisewest.com
(888) 851-8133

Crystal Cruises
www.crystalcruises.com
(888) 722-0021

Cunard Line
www.cunard.com
(800) 728-6273

Disney Cruise Line
www.disneycruise.com
(800) 951-3532

Holland America Line
www.hollandamerica.com
(877) 932-4259

Hurtigruten
(Formerly Norwegian Coastal Voyage Inc.)
www.hurtigruten.us
(866) 257-6071

Lindblad Expeditions
www.expeditions.com
(800) 397-3348

Majestic America Line
www.majesticamericaline.com
(800) 434-1232

MSC Cruises
www.msccruises.com
(800) 666-9333

Norwegian Cruise Line/NCL America
www.ncl.com
(866) 234-0292

Oceania Cruises
www.oceaniacruises.com
(866) 765-3630

Orient Lines
www.orientlines.com
(800) 333-7300

Princess Cruises
www.princess.com
(800) 774-6237

Regent Seven Seas Cruises
www.rssc.com
(877) 505-5370

RiverBarge Excursion Lines
www.riverbarge.com
(888) 462-2743

Royal Caribbean International
www.royalcaribbean.com
(866) 562-7625

Seabourn Cruise Line
www.seabourn.com
(800) 929-9391

SeaDream Yacht Club
www.seadream.com
(800) 707-4911

Silversea Cruises
www.silversea.com
(800) 722-9955

Star Clippers
www.starclippers.com
(800) 442-0551

Voyages of Discovery
(formerly Discovery World Cruises)
www.voyagesofdiscovery.com
(866) 623-2689

Windstar Cruises
www.windstarcruises.com
(800) 258-7245

About the Author

JIM WEST has logged millions of nautical miles as a cruise director and doles out the answers to cruise questions with wit and style. He has hosted a travel radio program, writes a travel column, and personally organizes and plans cruises for individuals and groups. Jim lives in Spring Valley, Illinois.

About the Updater

ANN CARROLL BURGESS, travel writer and naturalist lecturer, spends about four to five months each year aboard cruise ships lecturing and writing. Her other books include *The Guide to Western Canada,* published by The Globe Pequot Press. She writes actively for the Web and publications in both the United States and Canada.

Help Us Keep This Guide Up to Date

Every effort has been made by the author and editors to make this guide as accurate and useful as possible. However, many things can change after a book is published—establishments close, phone numbers change, facilities come under new management, etc.

We would love to hear from you concerning your experiences with this book and how you feel it could be made better and be kept up to date. While we may not be able to respond to all comments and suggestions, we take them to heart, and we also make certain to share them with the author. Please send your comments and suggestions to the following address:

The Globe Pequot Press
Reader Response/Travel Editorial Department
246 Goose Lane
Guilford, CT 06437
Or you may e-mail us at:
editorial@GlobePequot.com

Thanks for your input, and happy travels!

Notes

Notes

Notes

Notes